THE YOGA OF TRUE WEALTH

"I grew up loving sports, especially football. I reached the ultimate goal of playing in the NFL and winning a super bowl. That was not enough, nothing is ever enough for me. I needed and wanted another challenge, and I went into business. I have become very successful in my business. But that was not enough. Something was and is still missing. After reading *True Wealth* I feel like I am finally getting it. My journey is far from over, but thanks Fran, for helping me see the light. I will be working what you teach here until I get it right. Great book!"

—Super Bowl champion, All-Pro linebacker Phil Villapiano, Oakland Raiders #41

"I especially enjoyed your description of the roller coaster ride in which the individual buys when the market has gone up, and they assume it will go up further, and sell when the market has gone down and they assume that it will go down further."

—Dr. Harry Markowitz, American economist, recipient of the 1989 John von Neumann Theory Prize and the 1990 Nobel Memorial Prize in Economic Sciences.

"Anyone who has ever tapped into the Holy Energy to transform the material world around them will enjoy reading *The Yoga of True Wealth*. Francis Bitterly reminds us that uncommon wisdom, and ultimately wholeness, flows from hidden springs ... even on Wall Street."

—Luciano Siracusano, Chief Investment Strategist, WisdomTree Asset Management

"You cannot not benefit from the depth of wisdom revealed in this valuable book. The investment that Fran Bitterly made in his own growth from a very young age is a model to be admired. His story and insights are a gift to humanity. I have learnt so much, and am truly grateful to have been touched profoundly by Fran's breadth of caring and the expansive love in his heart."

—Robyn Stratton-Berkessel, Author and Speaker, positivitystrategist.com

"The genuineness of *The Yoga of True Wealth*, the authenticity and sincerity, the wonderfully inclusive merging of East and West, respecting the variety of spiritual approaches: Much impressed."

—Craig Canfield Psychotherapist

"*The Yoga of True Wealth* is the perfect fusion of material world practicality and Spiritual Truth. It comes at you from all different angles using the teaching of the masters (Buddha, Jesus, etc.)

"This book provides intellectual understanding of the wealth management business (concepts) and infuses spiritual truths to create an understanding that WEALTH is more than the money in our bank accounts.

"Peace of mind, Happiness, a sense of purpose, and helping other human beings are the real end game and building a stable financial life is one of the foundations to success and happiness."

—Jeffrey Silverman, Regional Recruiter, Willis Consulting, Inc.

"This beautiful book is who Fran really is and it very well may teach you who you really are. Fran's a spiritual warrior and his book will teach you about the true nature of reality and dissolving the Ego. *The Yoga Of True Wealth* will have you more persistently seeking God and will supply a common sense road map to soldier the road less traveled!"

—Dan Lattanzio, The Dan Program

"*The Yoga of True Wealth* sets the bar for what true holistic wealth management SHOULD mean. Bitterly does a masterful job of creating a road map teaching how to harness spirituality while incorporating the common messages of the greatest interfaith minds into our daily lives. The book is not solely about religion, finance or any other singular subject but instead weaves the universal framework for having a healthier mindset and existence."

—Andrew Tsiropinas, CIMA®, Regional Director—
WisdomTree Asset Management, Inc.

"A deeply moving and inspiring personal story, *The Yoga of True Wealth* will capture you with its authenticity. Rarely do we see a book deep in spiritual truths also getting the financial component right."

—John J. Bowen, Jr., Founder and CEO of CEG Worldwide, LLC, www.cegworldwide.com, #1 Business Coach for Financial Advisors

"Divine synchronicity occurred and I found myself reading Fran Bitterly's, *The Yoga of True Wealth*. As I read further along, page by page, I recognized with great appreciation this was a book with a true understanding about value, wealth, life, and the Grace that supports us all everyday; abundant and loving. There is so much to gain from this enlightened book; true wealth and what is real. I cannot recommend it enough."

—Janine L. Kimmel R.N. MTS, Author & artist of the award winning *The Magic Gown and The Yawning Rabbit River Chronicle*. www.JLKIMMEL.com

"With each passing year, I see more and more signs of the connectedness of all things. By attuning himself to the ineffable, Fran has found the resonant truth that lives within us all. And he shares that truth bravely, pointing us toward the way, the truth and the light. His is a journey worth sharing. And his light shines."

—Doug Pilley, Author

"Don't waste a minute of your time reading a single page of *The Yoga of True Wealth*—unless you're ready to make a shift in your thinking that can make you not only wealthier but even more important, happier! Francis has created a unique message that's filled with profound insights, clear in its intent and will emotionally hold your attention to get you to turn to the next page. Reading of 'THE GOD WHISPERER' and 'WHAT IS REAL WEALTH' will inspire you.

Nobody does a better job of combining the SPIRITUAL and FINANCIAL.

These are insights of a very wise man!"

— Joel Weldon, Hall of Fame Speaker, Golden Gavel Recipient, Executive Coach & Trainer
http://www.successcomesincans.com/

"How delightful to find Francis sharing everything from the life-saving spirituality of East and West to the wealth-saving knowledge of Modern Portfolio Theory. Here is a bounty of wisdom collected from stellar sages on the true wealth of Spirit—the glorious Divine Self, the God Who is Love—and how to be open for this single Life-Power to fully, freely live us. And from this 'peace that passes all understanding' found in truly letting go, letting God, one drops the self-defeating delusions and greed that cause suffering—and also ruin many approaches to investing."

—Timothy Conway, PhD, longtime spiritual teacher, author, counselor (and investor); Enlightened-Spirituality.org

"*The Yoga of True Wealth*, tackles the often taboo subject of wealth and religion. Whether you are Hindu, Buddhist, Jewish or Christian many will find this book a useful way to combine your faith principles and beliefs and your efforts to manage your wealth. Francis Bitterly tells his own compelling story of loss and struggle, financial and spiritual and uses it as a way to develop an 'Investment Theology.' Anyone interested in how their beliefs can work to help them with their financial objectives in life, will find this a good read."

—The Rev. K. Palmer Hartl, author of *The Ten Commandments of Management: Biblically inspired Methods to Success*

The Yoga of True Wealth:
Wisdom from a Heart on Wall Street

by Francis G. Bitterly, CFP®

© Copyright 2017 Francis G. Bitterly, CFP®

ISBN 978-1-63393-469-6

Published by

◄ köehlerbooks™

210 60th Street
Virginia Beach, VA 23451
800-435-4811
www.koehlerbooks.com

THE YOGA OF TRUE WEALTH

WISDOM FROM A HEART ON WALL STREET

FRANCIS G. BITTERLY, CFP®

VIRGINIA BEACH
CAPE CHARLES

DEDICATION

To my wife, Lisa, and my three beautiful daughters,
Alison, Catherine, and Caroline.
I love you more than words can tell.

TABLE OF CONTENTS

AUTHOR'S NOTE

This book tackles two very different and often separated subject matters: wealth management and spirituality. Although there are many books written on these matters individually, this book takes on both topics at the same time and interweaves them in the tapestry of my experience in the financial world and with the divine.

With this in mind, I have included my personal story from my own childhood to try and help the reader understand the reality of the subject matter being discussed.

Stories and myths have always been used by religions and cultures to try and describe the indescribable and point the way to "The Way." In the end, all are just like the finger pointing to the moon rather than the moon itself. The real truth is indeed within your own heart.

As a great song lyric from a legendary San Francisco band once stated, "that path is for your steps alone."

Chapters 1 through 3 introduce the reader to the main point of the book with the help of my personal childhood story, as well as my adolescence and young adulthood.

I realize that at some point along the path to spiritual growth, we all have to indeed abandon our own personal stories, for this is cargo that otherwise will weigh down the passenger unnecessarily.

Chapters 4 through 6 take the reader into metaphysical discussions, hoping to show common threads and universal truths of all of the great religions and wisdom traditions pointing to "The Way."

In this book, I often use common language associated with my own religion to show, over and over again, how these common threads connect.

Jesus's words, "the kingdom of heaven is within you," is one such example and is one of the most powerful messages of the book.

> Look no further than inside yourself.
> What is being sought is the seeker himself.

That also points to the paradoxical power of surrendering the Ego's personal identity.

Indeed, the great Tao of Lao Tzu, Jesus's Salvation, Buddha's Nirvana, and Krishna's Self-Realization cannot truly be understood by the Ego mind nor described by mere words. It is reserved for the private chambers of the human soul just beyond the mind and only found in a state of surrendered silence.

Chapters 7 and 8 are where I provide you with a general outline for how to start thinking about these spiritual concepts in terms of your own financial affairs, and how to cross them over to portfolio management and the wealth management process. These chapters are not to be viewed as individual investment advice, but merely as an outline for how to start thinking about managing an investment portfolio and following a disciplined wealth management process. With this in mind, I want you to keep your focus on the real treasure and prize of life itself: faith and love. I am aware that these chapters are a little different from the rest of the book, and heavy in financial content; however, if we keep the spiritual prize in mind, we can have even greater success in the wealth management process. More importantly, we will be happier and more grateful for all of our blessings.

Chapters 9 and 10 return you to the main point of the book, which is that what you are yearning for is closer than your own breath. It is here and now, within us, as the human heart and our own consciousness and spirit. What I am trying to bring to you is the simplicity of what we really are and ask you to wake up to this truth and see for yourself.

This awareness of consciousness itself (Spirit) is what all the great wisdom traditions throughout the ages have been trying to describe and point to.

This awakening takes place with the Ego mind's surrender to silence and with a new filling of this opened space with the alchemy of faith, love, and inspiration. In these chapters I also give some strategies to the reader to help bring this experience about.

"Know the Truth, and the truth shall set you free."

These words of Jesus are not referring to some foreign concept of faith. They are referring to the truth of what you are —beyond your titles, accomplishments, sorrows, personal story, name, body, mind, or any other form of any kind.

The message is: enjoy the beautiful dance of life, be successful in business, sports, investing, or whatever you do, but please, also be aware of something so freeing, liberating, and important —God is real.

God is everything.

God will help you and be revealed to you if you knock.

You are Spirit itself.

That art thou.

FOREWORD

The Yoga of True Wealth! The book the financial world has been waiting for!! Hallelujah!!!

Written from "a heart on Wall Street" nonetheless—could it get any better?

If ever there was a perfect time for this book to emerge, now is that time. Wall Street is under siege; just like everything else in the modern industrial world, it is creaking under the strain of a system in need of more heart. Literally millions of protestors all over the financial capitals of the modern world have risen up against a nonspecific enemy. United under an ancient banner screaming "Money is the root of all evil," they are reeling blindly, flailing like the mob storming the Bastille, baying for blood. Indeed these are troubled and uncertain times. A time of great revelation, shock and horror as not only the "have nots" stir in discontent, but also those of us who have—something is moving within us all.

It is that something to which this book alludes.

With eloquence and humility, honesty and heart, my dear friend Mr. Francis G. Bitterly has crafted a touching masterpiece replete with the deepest wisdom and most poignant truth. The fact that these golden threads are interwoven in the tapestry of his life unfolding makes it all the more medicine for the soul.

It is a beautiful story, as enlightening as it is touching—a blessing to the financial world from one of its own. Success, any great man will tell you, has never been exclusively about the acquisition of material wealth.

Petrodollars? Rubles? Yen or gold? It matters not if your soul you sold.

At last we have a delightful road map to navigate the road less traveled towards a future where perhaps the greatest riches await. Could it be that the essential missing ingredient in the whole financial industrial soup is about to be added in a liberal dose? That ingredient is nothing less than the human heart—the doorway to the eternal riches of the soul.

Welcome to the Yoga of True Wealth.

Dr. Nick Good
Kauai, Hawaii

PROLOGUE

Eyes of The World

"Right outside this lazy summer home
You ain't got time to call your soul a critic no
Right outside the lazy gate of winter's summer home
Wondering where the nut-thatch winters
Wings a mile long just carried the bird away"

"Wake up to find out that you are the eyes of the world,
the heart has its beaches, its homeland and thoughts of
its own.
Wake now, discover that you are the song that the
mornin' brings,
But the heart has its seasons, its evenin's and songs of
its own."[1]

OM

"Become loyal to your innermost truth.
Follow the Way when all others abandon it.
Walk the path of your own heart."

—Anonymous

---

1   See permission for "Eyes of the World" lyrics in Resources and Permissions
section of the book.

OUR SENSE OF CALLING:
THE STORY OF THE CARIBOU

The following is a beautiful writing by author and poet Mark Nepo. I felt it was a good explanation for my desire to write a book about spirituality. Even as I write this, I am aware of stepping out of my comfort zone in the process. I already have a great business, my clients appreciate me and are very loyal, so why would I want to write a spiritual book? Why should I risk being misunderstood or alienating clients due to my strong beliefs in spiritual concepts? Why not just write another conservative investment book? Possibly, Nepo's "Story of the Caribou" can explain my feelings of being called to write it.

"STORY OF THE CARIBOU"

"Every year, around the scalp of the planet, the caribou run the same path of migration along the edge of the Arctic Circle. They are born with some innate sense that calls them to this path. And every year, along the way, packs of coyote wait to feed on the caribou. And every year, despite the danger, the caribou return and make their way.

"Often nature makes difficult things very clear. What feels like confusion is frequently our human refusal to see things for what they are. What lesson do the caribou shout to us with the thunder of their hooves as they deepen the crown of the planet? They are evidence, even as we speak, of the fact that in every living thing there is an inner necessity that outweighs all consequence. For the caribou it is clear what it is.

"For spirits cried in human form, it is a blessing and a curse that we don't always know our calling. Part of our migration is the finding out. What is it we are called to, beneath all formal ambition? The caribou tell us that, though there are risks and dangers that wait in the world, we truly have no choice but to live out what we are born with, to find and work our path.

"These elegant animals bespeak a force deeper than courage, and, though some would call the caribou stupid, the mystery of their migration reveals to us the quiet, irrepressible emergence of living over hiding, of being over thinking, of participating over observing, of thriving over surviving.

"In regions near the Arctic, the caribou are not just seen as animals living out an instinct at all cost. Rather, it is believed that their endless run, no matter what stands in their way, is what keeps the Earth turning. And somewhere, beneath all hesitation and despair, it is our endless call to being, in each of us together, that keeps the fire at the center of the Earth burning."

Mark Nepo is a poet and philosopher who has taught in the fields of poetry and spirituality for 40 years. A *New York Times* number-one best-selling author, he has published 14 books and recorded eight audio projects. The "Story of the Caribou" is contained within his book, *The Book of Awakening: Having the Life You Want by Being Present to the Life You Have.*

THE YOGA OF TRUE WEALTH: WISDOM FROM A HEART ON WALL STREET

"Money is emptiness. When people who have money are trying to get ultimate security from the money, it's just impossible."

> —Tsoknyi Rinpoche, Tibetan Buddhist teacher
> and author

"No amount of money can make others speak well of you behind your back."

> —Chinese proverb

"I don't want to make money; I just want to be wonderful."

> —Marilyn Monroe

"A friend was visiting me and he said, 'Why do you have such a sour face?' I said, 'Well, I'm thinking about money.'"

> —Ram Dass, spiritual teacher and
> author of *Be Here Now* and *Be Love Now*

INTRODUCTION

"He that ruleth his spirit is greater than he that taketh a city."

—*Wisdom of Solomon*

Proverbs 16:32

I want you to be very honest with yourself. If you have opened this book, you know you have a higher purpose in life. You know this because despite your wealth, achievement, and success, something in you is not satisfied—perhaps even starving.

This fundamental sense of lack—which, deep down inside us, we all share—has been alluded to by every great spiritual teacher who has ever lived and is the root cause of all our stress, anxiety, and, believe it or not, disease.

The spiritual hunger, which nothing in the world can satisfy, has a source. Where that source is and how to fulfill it I have illustrated in this book, based on my own soul-shuddering and heart-opening journey.

"The greatest disease in the West today is not TB or leprosy; it is being unwanted, unloved, and uncared for. We can cure physical diseases with medicine, but the only cure for loneliness, despair, and hopelessness is love. There are

many in the world who are dying for a piece of
bread, but there are many more dying for a little
love. The poverty in the West is a different kind
of poverty—it is not only a poverty of loneliness
but also of spirituality. There's a hunger for love,
as there is a hunger for God."

—Mother Teresa, *A Simple Path*

Writing a book slowly became an objective of mine in my life over many years. Not immediately, of course, but after having some incredible life experiences—including the immeasurable and difficult loss of my mother when I was only four years old, overcoming a teenage alcohol battle, commuting to college at night to get a hard-fought-for education, and finally rising to the top of my field in the wealth management business—it became clear to me that I was ready. I had achieved what the world would consider a high level of success in the wealth management business by being named a Managing Director at my firm, a major Wall Street investment bank; and having been recognized by *Barron's* magazine five times as one of the top financial advisors in the country, I was also now considered an expert in my field. Some friends and family suggested that writing a book would be a natural for me.

It would have been easy just to write another investment book, but I didn't want to write a book that focused only on investing, wealth management, and financial planning. I felt I had a bigger message to convey, that being the real lessons and truth I had learned along the way. I wanted the book to include the struggles, pain, sorrows, surrendering, love, and, finally, joyful details and stories of my journey through what I now consider my spiritual awakening.

In our evolution toward inner peace we all face this struggle. Some have called this journey "the road less traveled." I believe we all will eventually have to journey down this path—we just may not realize it even as we are evolving.

The world is transforming. All of our sociopolitical and financial institutions are in a state of complete and utter transformation. The currents of life are becoming a raging flood, and millions of souls are being overwhelmed by the challenges of the times. I wanted the book to carry this message and include things happy, negative, positive, and excruciatingly sad. They all need to be incorporated into the overall message because I understand now that the message is bigger than just the usual financial discussion on the "do's and don'ts" of investing. Real wealth is beyond financial balance sheets, pie charts, asset allocation, and jargon that is difficult to understand. I can say this because I am confident I can help people to build wealth as the world would describe it. And I will admit that I've done it, and I have been successful at keeping it for my clients as well as for my family through difficult market cycles. But there is something even more important to understand and learn in life. I say this, too, because all of my life I have been searching for the answers to the big questions about overcoming sorrows and finding lasting peace, joy, and happiness. Over many periods in my life I have asked the bigger questions about why we are here and the true meaning and purpose of life. I have experienced how empty it can be living just from the ego or, as I will describe in this book, the small self, and living in the insecurity, fear, and sadness that goes along with this ego consciousness.

So what is the overall message I am bringing to this book?

It is the transformative message of finding real peace and joy by living in a surrendered, humble way and following God's will as taught by all of the great wisdom traditions, including the tenets taught by Jesus, Buddha, Krishna, *A Course in Miracles*, and other wisdom traditions of truth. The message is to let go of the ego in all affairs, to surrender to God's will, and to govern all actions, whether financial or otherwise, from the heart with love.

I know that I have a respected platform and career from which to speak this message.

Together, we will take a journey through life's experiences and navigate through them. We will also discuss the financial aspects of life, including building, protecting, preserving, and transferring wealth and how to do it with heart and love. More importantly, we will listen to the sounds of silence and hear the crucial lessons we can learn when we quiet our mind. But most importantly, we will discuss the great teaching of humility and love and how these pillars of humanism can help us not only have peaceful relations with family and friends, but also help us trust in the market's long-term history and trust in God's love while we are experiencing the consciousness of this life on earth.

At the end of each chapter I will endeavor to provide you with a simple meditation or contemplation, in the hope that you can experience how simple it is to let go of the ego and enjoy the boundless peace of the pure self that resides within us all. It is that part of you which truly nourishes the soul.

If you are ready to feed the part of you that no amount of materialism can fulfill and by doing so become the healthiest, happiest, and most successful you may have been for decades, then this book is for you.

Dissolve anxiety, step into the full power of your destiny, and join an enlightened group of like-minded individuals who are living life the way it's supposed to be lived by realizing the truth of the ages.

Everything you have been seeking for outside of yourself is already there inside you. All you have to do is accept it. If you are ready, this book is most definitely for you.

I hope you will find some quiet time to read, enjoy, and reflect on the words in my book. It was extraordinarily meaningful for me to write it for you. I wish you "eternal peace" as we begin this journey together.

Welcome to *The Yoga of True Wealth: Wisdom from a Heart on Wall Street*.

CHAPTER 1

Loss and Love

*Jesus said: "If those who lead you say to you:
See, the kingdom is in heaven, then the birds of
the heaven will go before you; if they say to you:
It is in the sea, then the fish will go before you.
But the kingdom is within you, and it is outside
of you. When you know yourselves, then you
will be known, and you will know that you are
the sons of the living Father. But if you do not
know yourselves, then you are in poverty, and
you are poverty."'*

—Gospel of Thomas 3

yo·ga\ˈyō-gə\noun

School of Hindu philosophy advocating and prescribing a course
of physical and mental disciplines for attaining liberation from
the material world and union of the self with the Supreme Being
or ultimate principle.

> *"Mankind is engaged in an eternal quest for
> that 'something else' he hopes will bring him*

happiness complete and unending. For those individual souls who have sought and found God, the search is over. He is that something."

—Paramahansa Yogananda

As I have walked down the path of my life, I have learned that life is a constant cycle of joy followed by pain and sorrow. But, through love and surrendering the will to God, we can all move through the pain and reach back to peace and joy.

It is an inner sort of "being" or living with that peace and love of God beyond understanding that is the ultimate goal in life. A member of The Beatles, George Harrison, once commented, "Everything else can wait, but the search for God cannot." Here we had one of the greatest rock stars in the world living in a humble, surrendered state of consciousness, the land of peace.

As we are growing up, we think it's other things that matter like the acceptance by our peers in social situations, getting into the right college, being in the right social group in high school, being popular or well-liked. The same things seem to matter after we start a family. We try to fill the empty well from the outside. Or we think the answer is choosing the right career and becoming a successful person in that career and being revered by others, being in the right groups, a member of the best club.

In reality, these things are just illusions, mere tricks our "small self" or ego play on us. We are caught up in the illusion of separation of the ego. You went to Harvard, I went to Rutgers. You are an American, I am a Russian. You are a Catholic, I am a Buddhist. You are a Democrat, I am a Republican.

All of these distinctions are how we identify ourselves and compare ourselves to others. They are mere words, not who we really are. They are clouds that blind us to the presence of peace, alive in the illusion of separation from God and others. Many times we fail to quiet the mind and its incessant comparisons and never-ending thinking. Our mind has a false sense of separation from God and thus a false sense of being God, and this keeps us from loving anywhere near our potential. This relates to loving others as well as loving ourselves.

"Your task is not to seek for love, but merely to seek and find all the barriers within yourself that you have built against it."

—*Jalaluddin Rumi*

"It makes no difference how deeply seated may be the trouble
How hopeless the outlook
How muddled the tangle
How great the mistake
A sufficient realization of love will dissolve it all
If only you could love enough
You would be the happiest
And most powerful being in the world"

—*Emmet Fox*

We are all together here; we just don't realize it.

I am going to take the peace beyond understanding and relate it to the investment process. I will show you how it's possible to find peace in your financial plan and in your life.

It starts within.

However, we may have to change the DNA of our belief systems. In order to really understand and "feel" the true meaning of life—to find our soul—we need to really challenge the deeply ingrained belief systems of separation from each other, as well as separation from God, that have clouded our vision. And we are going to see how to become the awareness behind our thought and begin to sense a great spiritual truth: We are not our thoughts. The true self is much bigger, vaster, and more permanent.

I will also relate these concepts back to investment psychology and explain why thinking too much can not only upset your life in general and destroy your inner peace, but it can also affect your long-term investment results.

MY MOTHER: THE GOD WHISPERER

I am not promoting any religion, sect, philosophy, or denomination. Much of the world has been in turmoil throughout history due to battles over religion and group ego. Instead, I am going to be discussing spirituality—not religion. I had to study Eastern philosophy, the great Buddha, and Hindu traditions to really come to a true understanding of the true wisdom of Christ within me. My hope is to share my journey and to point to some important signposts along the road so that you can find your own understanding deep within. And when you do, you will be finding your true self and soul.

I will be referring to Jesus, Buddha, Krishna, and others to help explain myself.

Jesus and the Buddha, as well as many other wisdom traditions, have often pointed to our need to be broken before we are open to awareness and growth. Jesus said in the Beatitudes, "Blessed are the poor in spirit for they will see the kingdom of heaven." He also said, "The kingdom of heaven is within you." We need to be broken open to the grace of humility and to ask God for help while searching within ourselves for answers. When this occurs, we are receptive to the growth and understanding that follows. We open to the truth within, and a whole new awareness comes to light.

> *"If you want to become whole*
> *First let yourself be broken*
> *If you want to become straight*
> *Let yourself be crooked*
> *If you want to become full*
> *Let yourself be empty*
> *If you want to be reborn*
> *Let yourself die*
> *If you want to be given everything*
> *Give everything up"*
>
> —*Lao-tzu, Tao Te Ching, translation by*
> *Stephen Mitchell*

With this surrendering comes the peace and power beyond understanding. I am going to take you along my path to freedom and help you reach yours as well. We will reflect on the losses, trials, sorrows, and forks in the roads, the major obstacles and life lessons along the path, and find real peace and knowingness. We will talk about investment strategy and the institutional investment process as well.

Do you remember waking up to the concept of consciousness, of "being conscious"? Most of us don't remember exactly what we were doing or when this occurred, but mine really began in the presence of my mother. In my case, they are my only memories of her.

When I was a very young boy, and my mother was dying of cancer, she would whisper and teach me things. I now call her the God Whisperer. I am convinced that her early life lessons, taught to me when I was three and four, helped me to survive in this world and develop my experience of the grace of God I have enjoyed in my life. Her outpouring of pure love stayed with me as she planted the seeds of grace. She interceded in my life during my darkest nights of the soul.

And she taught me through her actions, as well. For example, I remember her taking food to the Monsignor at St. Anthony's Church while she was very sick. She was so devoted that every day she continued to take bags of food for the poor and attended Mass. Even though she was dying, she would still teach me things that didn't seem so important at the time, but I finally understood. Now I realize everything she taught made a lot of sense. What she was whispering was about love. Love is real and from God. Our love could not be separated by death. Your heart is what is important and to live life from the heart.

One night, when she must have known it would not be long before our physical separation, she and I were outside looking up at the sky, and she explained to me that someday we would swing on a star together. I used to think this was a fairy tale. Now I understand the beauty of her foresight and faith.

MERRILY, MERRILY, MERRILY, MERRILY . . .
LIFE IS BUT A DREAM

I never understood the cosmic nature of what she was talking about when I was a child, but now I understand a lot more about the metaphysical nature of her words. Having had a spiritual awakening beginning as a 21-year-old, I now understand what she was trying to tell me.

Our bodies are actually made up of condensed energy, very similar to outer space and starlight. My mother taught me about love at a very young age. She taught me that speaking from the heart and into the heart is what is meaningful and real in this world.

In the book *A Course in Miracles*, the premise is "Nothing real can be threatened. Nothing unreal exists. Herein lies the peace of God." This is also what the great Eastern philosophies convey, whether it be Buddhism or Hinduism. It took me studying all the great wisdom traditions before I really understood my own childhood faith and the true wisdom of Jesus Christ and His teaching and transformative message.

I also remember how my mother would sing to me. She would sing the sweet children's song "Row, Row, Row Your Boat." And as it continues, "Merrily, merrily, merrily, merrily, life is but a dream." Today, I sense the truth of those words and her awareness to the true nature of reality here on earth. You see, life really is much like a dream. Many never awaken to it. But we are so full of our own perceptions and inherited instincts and illusions that we can't escape the dream.

Jesus spoke of it. So did Krishna and Buddha.

When my mother died, I was in such pain, and my nose was buried in the couch for a month. What could be worse? I quietly and slowly came out of it when my father finally remarried. He really had to, as we were not going to school. There were five boys in the family, and I was the youngest. My father had to leave the house every day at 6:15 to go into Manhattan for his job. My brother and I were shipped off to relatives, and experienced four or five different school systems.

It was agony. I couldn't read until I was in third grade, and I really didn't even know how to hold a pencil. So my dad got remarried, and things finally began to settle down. The first year in the new school was still hell, and I always cried as I was brought to the school bus by my stepmother. I was heartbroken. I slowly adjusted and finally began to find friends, play sports, and be a kid like most normal children.

But my mother had been my whole world, and I can still remember most everything about her. It's like the soul is alert when it has certain experiences, and I have memories that are very vivid from an age when most people aren't aware of being conscious. When it comes to my mother and my childhood, I remember everything.

One day in 1965, one of my older brothers was home from school, and I began kicking at him, just fooling around and not hurting him, and he lifted my leg up and flipped me! Unfortunately, it was a hard fall, and I ended up breaking my collarbone and crawling into the bed with my mother, who was very, very sick that evening. I just remember how comforting it was and how she took most of the hurt away. This was the night I remembered her singing, "Row, row, row your boat, gently down the stream."

As I mentioned, she was the God Whisperer, and she whispered about love and faith and most times without uttering a word. Of course, words are simply a way of communicating, but there are communication levels that are beyond language. They're universal, and that's why the great Yogis of India will stare into your eyes or you'll stare at them without speaking. There is no need for words. And everything is understood. The great Indian sage Ramana Maharshi was amazing. When people would visit him, many times he wouldn't say a word. He was totally self-realized. Yet your heart would open up just to be in his presence.

I can't help but believe that my mother communicated on this level as well; she was very spiritual and was of spirit because she knew she was dying, but she was full of love and faith and radiating a divine presence. She continued teaching me things— her way of preparing me for the life I would have to live without her.

One night, my brother and I were invited to have dinner with some friends up the street. After dinner, I remember watching

TV in their basement, and I can still recall small details like where the TV was positioned—on the right side of me as opposed to the left side of me. Later that evening on March 7, 1966, my older brother picked us up and walked us home from our friend's house, and he said, "You know, Mom's not going to live forever." My brother and I broke away from our hand-holding, and we bolted home—I knew instinctively when my brother uttered those words that my mother had passed. I was four years and 11 months old. I ran into the house and looked around the room where her hospital bed had been, and everything was gone. Nothing was in her room, and I realized immediately that my mother was gone as well. There was no question in my young mind that she went on to heaven that night. I thought all of her clothes and belongings, which were nowhere to be seen, had left and gone to heaven as well.

I had to sit with that reality and just had to go through it. Love is the only thing that can take the place of that reality. The night my mom died . . . to me, it was the loss of a lifetime, the awakening to the need to find a way to transcend the world. My life would never be the same.

THE LOSS OF LOVE . . . BUT ON WITH MY JOURNEY

As I continued on my youthful journey after my mother's death, I had to cope with a new family and stepmother a year later and then the experience of not wanting to go to school, being brought to the bus stop in tears, crying in class, and having to have my stepsisters come into my class to urge me to eat lunch. I was totally emptied by the loss of love. I felt like I was a subpar human being. This may sound odd, but one time when I got a new pair of pants, I felt that the pants didn't realize that I was going to have to wear them. I literally had that conversation in my mind.

One other time, I went to a birthday party for a friend up the street before my dad got remarried; I had made a present for the birthday girl. I literally took one of my father's shavers, put it in a box and gift-wrapped it for her. I wasn't thinking that this was a dangerous present; it was just all that I could come up with. Without a mother, there really is confusion over such events. But you can only imagine how surprised she was when she opened up the box. I was very embarrassed and confused. I really had no one to tell me whether it was right or wrong. As the other kids laughed at me, I realized that I just wanted my mother back. Why was I so different? Why did I feel so empty inside? It would be many years until I had answers to many of these questions.

We are complicated individuals, and we can get so far away from that quiet, true self that we can easily forget it's there. We drift far away from the stillness and the sound of silence. Not only do we forget, but also we never know in many cases that it even exists. Joseph Campbell, American scholar, talked about the "Hero's Journey" in his book *The Hero with a Thousand Faces.* He said as we go through life, experience pain and then sorrow, and come out of it somehow, there is something inside of us all the while that helps—it's that quiet voice, that quiet piece of us that is eternal, and it's always been there, and it will always be there.

Some people call it the soul; some people call it the spirit or the eternal eye. It's beyond description but everyone is reaching for this, and they don't know it. I was striving for this at a very young age.

We will discuss this and relate it back to wealth management as well. We will strive for that level of consciousness so you get into the great stream of life, living from your heart. "Merrily, merrily, merrily, merrily, life is but a dream."

You inhale God's love . . . you exhale, surrendering to God's peace and love in the present moment.

> *"Everything else can wait, but the search for God cannot."*
>
> —*George Harrison*

Box of Rain

"Walk into splintered sunlight
Inch your way through dead dreams
to another land
Maybe you're tired and broken
Your tongue is twisted
with words half spoken
and thoughts unclear
What do you want me to do
to do for you to see you through
A box of rain will ease the pain
and love will see you through"[2]

CONTEMPLATION

Consider deeply the loss or losses you have experienced in your life, whether it be the loss of a loved one, your health, even a cherished pet. Then consider the hidden gifts the challenge eventually brought into your reality Just close your eyes, and deeply contemplate the experience and the wisdom you gleaned, what life gave you as you integrated or adapted to new circumstances. While doing this, get in touch with the part of you that witnessed and experienced the loss. It is the same part of you witnessing and experiencing these words. Feel it. Feel it with the beauty of tenderness. Allow yourself to feel the pure awareness that exists eternally at the core of your being. Put the book down, take a few soft gentle breaths, and reflect deeply now.

---

2   Permission for "Box of Rain" lyrics in Permissions and Resources section in the back of the book.

CHAPTER 2

The Journey to Liberation

"And know that I am with you always; yes, to the end of time."

—*Jesus Christ*

"Liberation is our natural, free, spiritual condition, minus all the harsh conditions of material nature."

—*Krishna*

"You can search throughout the entire universe for someone who is more deserving of your love and affection than you are yourself, and that person is not to be found anywhere. You yourself, as much as anybody in the entire universe, deserve your love and affection."

—*Buddha*

I talked about the loss of love in Chapter 1 and shared with you my experiences as a young boy. I also shared the stories of my mom, whom I called the God Whisperer, and why I believed she was. But I must continue with my story and tell you about the day I almost died and about how several experiences had a profound effect on me and literally changed my life. It was the beginning of my journey to liberation.

As I said, it was a good thing my father remarried. My brothers and I were home alone all the time, and that gave us an opportunity to act like boys—and my older brothers were beginning to have beer parties! My oldest brother was 11 years older than I was, so it seemed like my brothers had beer parties all the time. It was the 1960s. My brother and I didn't even go to school most of the time.

I remember once I was met in front of my house by two teenage girls when I was being dropped off by the school bus. They intercepted me and took me downtown to get a milkshake, and I was wondering why. They were keeping me from seeing the police at the house. My older brothers and their friends had just had their party interrupted at the house by the township police, and they were brought down to the station for questioning. That was the environment in which we were living, and it really forced my dad to get remarried. He tried to have nannies watch over us, but the situation was out of his control. This is why he had to send my brother and me away to live with different relatives on various occasions before he got remarried.

After he remarried, we all moved into one house like *The Brady Bunch*. There were eight of us now. There were five boys in my family, and my stepmom had three girls. We began to live a pretty normal life. I had some good friends and was having a lot of fun playing sports. One night, my brother asked me if I wanted to do a sleep-out with his older friends—with hot dogs and hamburgers by a campfire. I really wanted to, and our stepmother said it was okay. I was about nine years old and weighed 80 pounds soaking wet when I was introduced to alcohol that night. We drank Boone's Farm apple wine, and I loved it. Then we all snuck into the drive-in theater where *Love Story* was playing.

Needless to say, I got very drunk that night, was carried out of the woods the next morning, and made it home after being dunked in the creek on the way to get clean (I had thrown up all over my clothes). But a week later, I was at a Pop Warner football practice, and I was thinking about what happened that night, with the movie and all of the drinking and all of the things that had gone on . . . and a thought crossed my mind. That was really fun; when can I do that again? I believe I was actually born with an inherent alcohol problem. To have a fantasy about drinking just one week after being terribly sick was absolute insanity. And, indeed, this is how many people go through life.

When the coast was clear and I thought there was an opportunity, I would try to drink. There were times when I would get caught by my parents, and they would punish me, for example, by not letting me play in my town's PONY league at the Mayor's Trophy baseball game. Or perhaps they would let me play three innings, and I would be forced to leave the game and come home. But at one point, I really believed there was something different in my DNA—because I wanted to drink whenever I could sneak away.

The summer sleep-outs in the woods were the solution, they were where I was able to let loose. From the age of 12 onward, I was able to secure the freedom to drink. We slept fireside under the stars and had great times. I can still remember all of the hit music of the summer of 1973 that played in the background, music by Paul Simon, The Beatles, The Allman Brothers Band, the Grateful Dead.

We were deep in the woods. We cooked, we drank, we laughed, we did not sleep. One beautiful summer night at around 9:30 p.m., we were sitting by the fire drinking when up the path came the most frightening sight I had ever seen in my life: Three large figures wearing scuba diving masks were coming our way, each holding flames in front of them. They were walking like they were right out of a horror movie. We all left our drinks and the fire and ran deep into the woods as far as we could go, banging through trees until the sticker bushes and forest would not allow us to go any farther. I had never been, and still have never been, more scared in my entire life.

As I rested there standing up, but on an angle at which the woods had stopped my forward motion, my heart almost exploded with fright. It seemed like days until the sound of hard laughter finally came across my consciousness. It occurred to me this may have been the work of the "T Crew," as we called them. They were the older kids of the neighborhood, the kids I played baseball and football with as an eight-year-old and the same kids who taught us about Woodstock—what it meant to be a hippie, rock and roll—and who had also handed me my first drink years earlier. They were now laughing it off and drinking our liquor. They were the coolest guys in town, and on this night they gave us little kids a scare we would never forget. I did not really drink very much or hang out late the rest of the year (except summer) until I was sixteen and a half, out of fear of severe punishment from my stepmother. But those many summer nights under the stars were the times of my life that I will never forget.

When I was a junior in high school, my parents asked me why I wasn't going out like the other kids, and I told them, "Because if I come home with a beer on my breath, you are going to punish me."

They said, "Oh, it's okay if you have a beer or two."

Well, that's pretty much all I needed to hear. That was when the partying really took off, and within a year after I had graduated from high school, I looked back at high school and childhood as the "glory days," thinking those were the good times. Life after high school had gotten very gray, all of a sudden.

It seemed drinking was different for me, because any time I had a beer, I got drunk. I actually went through a very dark period. It's what St. John of the Cross called in his treatise the "Dark Night of the Soul," which was written in 1578 while he was imprisoned by his Carmelite brothers. St. John narrates the journey of the soul from its bodily home to its union with God. The journey is called "The Dark Night" because darkness represents the hardships and difficulties the soul meets in detachment from the world and reaching the light of the union with the Creator. And that is exactly how I felt at the time. I didn't drink every day. Sometimes I would go weeks without drinking, but whenever I had one drink, I was pretty much going to get drunk. I had a compulsion once alcohol entered my bloodstream.

About the same time, my dad's brother was staying with us. Previously, he had a seat on the New York Stock Exchange, and when I was growing up, it seemed like he had a new Cadillac and a new Lincoln every year. Unfortunately, he also had an alcohol problem. He had been struggling and was living in California. My dad eventually tracked him down and brought him back from California, and I gave him my bedroom. I was about 18, and I believe that's when I became aware of the dangers of alcohol. He had been sober for 20 years before his last drunk took him to California away from his family. After he returned, he got sober again and never had another drink during his life's final 30 years. I went out, and I taste-tested for a couple years. I wanted to see if I could have a beer without getting drunk. But I could never do it. I never could have a sip without getting drunk.

So I was in a kind of purgatory from ages 18 to 21. I was suffering. I lost my driver's license due to drunk driving, and I was heading down the wrong path. When I was 19, I experienced a life-threatening auto accident. I was a passenger in a car coming home from a beer party. The car I was in missed the turn in the road and flew off into the woods. I was thrown from the car after it hit a tree—it had gone 80 miles an hour into the woods, and I got ejected by the impact. Then it hit two more trees and came to rest right on my chest. I woke up from that frightening accident by the grace of God. I remember opening my eyes, looking straight ahead and reading the word "Uniroyal," which was on the tire that was resting on my chest.

As it turned out, I broke my back and my ankles, had emergency surgery for blood clots in my stomach, and spent more than a month in the hospital. I was one eighth of an inch from being paralyzed from my back injuries. These were the dark days, and this is where that partying trail led me. I had almost died!

Man hospitalized after crash

EATONTOWN— Francis Bitterly, the 19-year-old son of Councilman Paul Bitterly, is in the intensive care unit of Monmouth Medical Center, Long Branch, with injuries sustained when a car from which he was thrown landed on top of him early yesterday.

A hospital spokesman last night had no report on Bitterly's condition. He was the passenger in a car driven by ███████████ 19, of Tinton Falls, who is listed in satisfactory condition at the hospital.

According to Patrolman John Paulus, Bitterly suffered a back injury, broken leg and cuts and bruises on his face. ████████ suffered a laceration on his face, a broken nose and several cuts and bruises.

According to Paulus, ████████'s car was traveling east on Wyckoff Road at approximately 80 miles per hour when it went out of control and struck a tree, throwing Bitterly from the vehicle, Paulus said.

The car spun around a tree, flew six feet into the air before striking another tree, and slid down the tree onto Bitterly's chest, Paulus said. The accident occurred at about 1:15 a.m.

Bitterly was pinned under the car for approximately 10 minutes, Paulus said. One of the first aidmen who came to the scene used a hydraulic jack to lift the car off of Bitterly.

The Eatontown Motor Vehicle Extraction Unit was called in to rescue ██████ who was trapped in the car.

Both men were transported to Monmouth Medical by the First Aid Squad.

████████ was issued a summons for careless driving. His is scheduled to appear in municipal court on Oct. 16.

That was the gravest moment, the "almost didn't make it home alive" experience, but I knew I had to deal with my problem. I turned my life over to the care of a higher power, and I surrendered my problems to God's will. I was finally able to trust in love again. When I was out there partying all the while, I had this feeling that I wasn't being true to myself, that I wasn't living the way God wanted me to, and that silence was inside of me that tells us there is a better way. It told me that I had to stop doing certain things and start trusting God and that He would take care of me. I was praying to my mother in heaven and asking for her help. The grace of God was in my heart. Of course, that was the "larger" self, the divine soul's yearning, not the "small" self talking. The small self is connected to the ego and connected to that insatiable desire that Buddha talks about as the main cause of suffering.

> *"Do not let your hearts be troubled. Trust in God; trust also in me."*
> —*Jesus Christ*

You see, we are under the illusion that we are separate, that we are this little island separate from everybody else in a big ocean, and inside we are scared out of our wits until we realize that deep within, we are all an inseparable part of the ocean. Our life journey is like a beautiful river returning to the realization that we are that ocean.

The Hindus call this soul island the Jiva. If we trust in God's higher guidance—the cosmic or pure consciousness, or the universal continuum that we begin tapping into as we become more conscious of the subtle depth of ourselves—we then get the power we need to live in peace. It all leads to the same altar. I think we have to go through a lot of pain until we open up and start that part of the journey to liberation and freedom.

> *"Your pain is the breaking of the shell that encloses your understanding. Even as the stone of the fruit must break, that its heart may stand in the sun, so must you know pain.*
> *And could you keep your heart in wonder at*

*the daily miracles of your life, your pain would
not seem less wondrous than your joy; and you
would accept the seasons of your heart, even as
you have always accepted the seasons that pass
over your fields. And you would watch with
serenity through the winters of your grief. Much
of your pain is self-chosen. It is the bitter potion
by which the physician within you heals your
sick self.*

*Therefore, trust the physician, and drink his
remedy in silence and tranquility: For his hand,
though heavy and hard, is guided by the tender
hand of the Unseen, and the cup he brings,
though it burn your lips, has been fashioned of
the clay which the Potter has moistened with His
own sacred tears."*

—*Kahlil Gibran, The Prophet*

We have to reach a point of surrender. That is what Jesus's message was, that's what Buddha taught, and that's what Krishna taught. It's all universal truth, and, in reality, it is the same thing with investments, assuming you follow the right strategies in terms of approach like Modern Portfolio Theory, asset allocation, diversification, and so on.

We always seem to think we know where our feet are going at any one time, to control the grass that is growing under our feet. This is where the wonderful Buddhist thinking comes in when they talk about impermanence. Nothing is permanent. You can't hold onto things forever. At the end of the day, nothing is real except for love. Much of what we are disturbed about at any moment in time is really mere nonsense, it's all an illusion, it's all a cloud, it's all smoke and mirrors. If we could only see other people's souls, and if we could see through our own self-centered reflection of who we think people are, we would see them the way God sees them—we wouldn't be judging them, we wouldn't be hating them, we wouldn't be feeling the way we feel. The way to get above it and deal with what Joseph Campbell talked about in his book—and what Buddha and Christ and Krishna and all the great avatars talked about—is to change the perception of who you are looking at and to see yourself. That's why those spiritual actions work. When you love others, you love yourself; when you hate others, you're really only hating yourself.

We need to return to love in our lives. Author Marianne Williamson talks about this in her book, *A Return to Love: Reflections on the Principles of a Course in Miracles.* Williamson shares her reflections on *A Course in Miracles* and her insights on the application of love in the search for inner peace. She discusses how love is a potent force, the key to inner peace, and how, by practicing love, we can make our own lives more fulfilling. We need love to keep our families together, and you might not realize it, but we also need love in wealth management. I am eager to share this concept with you in upcoming chapters.

> *"The true profession of man is finding his way to himself."*
> —Herman Hesse

CONTEMPLATION

Consider deeply your own personal "dark night of the soul" and how it affected you. What were the most powerful lessons you learned? How did it affect your values? Have there been times in your life when you have chosen love over ego, and times when you have not? What were the differences in the outcome of those experiences? Consider how they have affected you. Are there any relationships or situations in your current reality that would benefit from more love and less ego? Where are they? Who are they? Consider deeply before reading on how you can bring more peace into these dynamics.

Take a few soft gentle breaths. Put the book down. Drop in again to that pure feeling of awareness, and allow the imagination its freedom and peace.

Trust.

Breathe.

Enjoy.

CHAPTER 3

Lonely Days of Determination

"No one knows what he can do until he tries."

—Publilius Syrus

Like a Life-Giving Sun

 "You could become a great horseman
And help to free yourself and this world
Though only if you and prayer become
Sweet Lovers.
It is a naive man who thinks we are not
Engaged in a fierce battle,
For I see and hear brave foot soldiers
All around me going mad,
Falling on the ground in excruciating pain.
You could become a victorious horseman
And carry your heart through this world
Like a life-giving sun
Though only if you and God become
Sweet Lovers."

—Hafiz

In the previous chapter, I mentioned that after my father remarried, things became very different. I lived with my stepmother, three new sisters, and one of my brothers because my father lived in my old house with my older brothers until we sold that house. I seldom saw my dad or my older brothers. The winter of 1967 was one of sadness and despair for me. Not only had I lost my mom a year earlier, but now I was in a new family, a new house, and a new school system. It took me a long time to settle down in this new environment.

Finally by September, 1968, our new house was built, my dad sold his house in Lincroft, and we all moved into a house in Eatontown, New Jersey. This new family was how I grew up. In reality, the marriage lasted about 10 years. My father and stepmother grew apart, and divorce was in the air by my senior year of high school. My stepmother was in a position financially to force my dad and me out of the house shortly after my high school graduation.

Today, I hold absolutely no animosity toward my stepmother and stepsisters. They were doing the best they could do in a difficult situation. At one time, I was very angry and hurt by a lot of what happened with our family. Today, I love my stepmother and stepsisters and often ask God to help us all to love and forgive each other. I have not seen them in 36 years.

Despite this and other challenges, my father always had a wonderful and loving heart. Every day before school he would put vitamins on the table for me and a little bit of money for lunch. He was a beautiful man, and he did a great job of raising me. He always corrected my speech to help me be a better communicator. He watched me play sports, especially in my senior year of high school.

One of my greatest memories of my dad watching me play sports was on a beautiful summer night in 1976. I was 15. My dad was on crutches, and he came to the game anyway. He sat humbly by himself as many of the other dads yelled and were very involved. We faced a hard-throwing, excellent pitcher this night, and he struck out the first two batters on six pitches. The first pitch he threw me I drilled into the beautiful blue moist July air, eclipsing the space 100 feet above the two outfielders. As I came back to the bench after rounding the bases, I stopped to kiss my father squarely on the cheek as he clapped in appreciation and joy for my home run. It was a rare moment in childhood when all the stars had aligned and time seemed to stand still. He was so humble about his son's sports accomplishments, but on this night everyone got to know who my dad was. I often think about what might have happened with my playing baseball had it not been for my desire to party at a young age. On this particular night, the unique possibility of childhood and father and son seemed to be perfectly arranged in love, nature, and joy, and somehow time really was suspended. I know now it is eternal and buried in my heart. The love was always there—there was never a doubt—and that is really what kept everything stable for me.

But he had some health issues, and those, combined with some financial issues, caused us to eventually lose the house. We had to move into an apartment after my stepmother took over the house. During the hard times in the marriage, it even got to the point where we were actually splitting the space inside the refrigerator, separating the boys' food from the girls' food. It was difficult, but somehow we managed.

It is always darkest before the dawn and, as I mentioned earlier, I had to go through my dark night of the soul from age 18 to 21. But soon after that, I made a decision to turn my life over to God.

THE POWER OF FAITH AND SURRENDER

Jesus told them:

> *"I tell you the truth, if you had faith even as small as a mustard seed, you could say to this mountain, 'Move from here to there,' and it would move. Nothing would be impossible."*

> *—Matthew 17:20*

When I was in my greatest despair and darkest hour the day after my last night out drinking on October 1, 1982, I had a "mustard seed" of faith experience. As I paced in my home, remorseful at the hopelessness of not being able to stop doing something that I so badly wanted to stop doing, I cried out to God in despair, surrendering my will finally, in totality. Before this experience, I felt I had been cheated in life not only because of losing my mother at a young age or because of the pain of my car accident, but I also felt I had been cheated in life because I had suffered with my alcohol problem. This indeed was a problem that would stand in the way of me starting my adult life.

As I cried in the bathroom after being sick to my stomach, I noticed a wooden painting of Jesus's mother, Mary, holding her son. The wood painting startled me. I never really noticed it or given it much thought before. My eyes glared at it. In that moment, I called on what little bit of faith I had left in me. I begged this piece of wood with this painted image of a mother holding her son to please help me. I begged and prayed to Jesus through his mother Mary for help. Although it is difficult to put into words, today I know I was blessed and touched by the grace of God at that moment.

I still have this wood painting in my bedroom today. It represents to me the power of faith and the power of the grace of God. My life has been nothing short of a miracle since that day. I have been blessed with so many gifts and joys. I have been given the grace of God in all my affairs, my beautiful wife and three daughters being among my most precious. Yet today, as I look back at all of the material forms and physical matter that have been manifested in my life since that day in 1982, I know that the greatest gift of all I have received is the formless gift of the spirit of love and faith in God.

The peace that passeth all understanding.

Nothing else compares to this. The grace of God for me today is the returning home to the Holy Spirit and the returning to the home I came from.

This is what this book is about. This is the gift I am hoping to share with you in this book. Gloria in Excelsis Deo.

> *"Amazing grace! how sweet the sound*
> *That saved a wretch like me!*
> *I once was lost but now am found,*
> *Was blind but now I see."*
>
> — *John Newton, author of* Amazing Grace

> *"I have set before thee an open door, and no man can shut it."*
> —*Revelation 3:8*

Shortly after this experience, I also made a decision that I wanted to get serious about my education and all the other areas and aspects of my life.

TRUCKIN' UP TO NEW BRUNSWICK

My commute to Rutgers University in New Brunswick from Eatontown in Monmouth County was very challenging, and the drive took about an hour each way. My dad and I were roommates while I commuted to college, and again he was very supportive. He had a very serious leg injury, and he suffered greatly. I would go to the store and get food for us, and we were on a fixed budget. His love and perseverance in life despite very few good nights of sleep, the continued hospital stays, and persistent, excruciating pain were a life lesson in itself. His love was absolutely unconditional. I had classes twice a week from 8 a.m. until 11 p.m. There were times during the winter when I feared that my ability to attend class would be derailed due to snowstorms that could potentially endanger my commute. But I was able to overcome many obstacles in my way, and it was basically due to the love and grace of God. And, of course, the love of my father. The courage to continue came from God. I could not have done it without that grace. My father continued to be very supportive, even with few resources.

Getting an education was a big deal for me. I really wasn't all that well educated when I started at Rutgers. I had to learn many of the basics, plus study math, and I also had to gain a lot of emotional intelligence to get started on my new path. Then I eventually studied business, economics, finance, and markets, and it really came together for me. But I can say with certainty that it was through no power of my own; it was all power from a higher source, courage from something that I had turned my life over to. It was not so much religion as it was a force of goodness which seemed to seep into every inch of my consciousness following my complete surrender to it. My intuition was like never before.

Along the way, I had a challenging course. It was a literary study of the New Testament: going into it, I thought I had all the answers to all the religions. It spun my head around a little because I thought it was going to be an easy class, since I thought I knew so much already. I had read the Bible earlier, during my awakening, but this was a very difficult course based on the Synoptic Gospels of Matthew, Mark, Luke, and John. There were many contradictions. The challenges were such that I was questioning whether the rock to Jesus' tomb was moved, or how the Gospel stories literally contradicted themselves in some places. I thought the teacher was an atheist, though I later found out he was a Baptist minister.

Nonetheless, the course was designed to challenge the student to the core. I recovered quickly, however, and later my faith grew stronger from the challenge. But I had to let go of the intellect and again surrender to the intuition. When this occurred, I felt the power return, and I could sense the peace of unconditional knowingness without having all of the intellectual religious answers.

As you can imagine, my early college sobriety had its own challenges. On one difficult day, I had an amazing experience when taking a statistics course. It was during a test, and I was really concentrating on doing well. My mind just froze. Of course, I didn't do well on the test because I froze up and I walked out of the class in tears. I'll never forget it. I was on College Avenue, just wandering around, and I happened to see my Labor Relations teacher, a nice African American gentleman.

Earlier in the semester during classes I had been always the conservative business management student arguing with him in class, taking the side of management against his labor union tilts. Obviously my ego was at work in class. On the day of my statistics test meltdown, he saw me, noticed I was in distress, and he put his arm around me, calmed me, and quoted a passage from the Bible. He quoted Jesus:

> *"Come to me all you who labor and are heavy laden, and I will give you rest, take my yoke upon you and learn from me, for I am gentle and lowly in heart, and you will find rest in your souls."*

> —Matthew 11:28

It was like running into my mother on College Avenue. The God Whisperer herself. I think he really understood me because he shared that he had also stopped drinking a long time ago. I had told him of my drinking problem and my fear of the test. I truly believe that this was a case of the hand of God touching me at a time when I needed it most, the intervention of Grace. I'll never forget that moment. Thinking about it often, I believe he was like a guardian angel because that was a very important time in my life. I could have quit right then and there and gone to the student center Pub for pitchers of beer. The point is, that teacher was my brother and my mother and the hand of God's grace all wrapped in one message. There was no reality to the notion of a difference between labor or management, no separation in the true eyes of God. We have a choice of how we hear the reality around us. It can be either a lesson for higher consciousness or an excuse to sink back into the ego's need to feed itself, like a parasite eating away at our God-given right to peace—the quiet eternal Self or universal consciousness, Atman, Buddha nature, or Christ consciousness, what you call it is your business—knowing it is there and tapping into this peace is what is important.

On the last day of college, driving home on Route 18 in New Jersey, I cried. I always have trouble talking about my college experience without welling up with tears, because I have been so blessed in so many ways. It was great joy, but an amazing struggle, to complete college, especially when you see where I was three years into it before surrendering to God. But that last day was very emotional for me as I was driving back, looking at the red sky above. A voice spoke to my conscience that I had heard so many times before: "I can do all things through Christ who strengthens me." The God Whisperer was smiling down on her son. We were beginning to swing on the stars.

NOTHING REAL CAN BE THREATENED. NOTHING UNREAL EXISTS. THEREIN LIES THE PEACE OF GOD

Summing up my college experience, it was a wonderful challenge, and I was so grateful to have completed my goals. I received my diploma, but didn't go to the graduation. I really had no desire or motivation to get in the car again and take the drive up to Rutgers, and being that no one really knew me well or would miss me there, I celebrated with my close friends, my father, and my close sense of the Holy Spirit that had guided me and that was now always with me. I also had to get right to work. I had known all along I wanted to be a Financial Advisor. It had taken me three and a half years to get 18 college credits before I stopped drinking, and I had now finished college in two and one-half years. My grade point average had gone from a C—to an A.

I was 23 when I entered the financial services industry and passed the Series 7 test right away within 6 weeks, having studied 11 hours a day in a basement. Within two months, I was a Registered Representative. I wasn't too proud; I would work until 9 p.m. cold-calling people, prospecting by mail, trying everything to gain potential clients. I would go home, eat, read research, and then pray. My prayers were now prayers of gratitude. Thank you, God. Thank you for helping me to stop drinking. Thank you for allowing me to survive my car accident. Thank you for helping me pass the Series 7 exam. Thank you for putting me on earth and, my personal God prayer to Jesus, thank you for being my sacrifice. I had no real connections, so I just tried to visualize my goals and manifest the dreams so I could be what I wanted to become. I now had certainty that anything was possible with faith. Today, I realize God was always the doer. His power can do miracles. I had to battle with the fact that I had no clients and obviously I needed them, but again, I used prayers and God as my strength. I had trouble sleeping at times because the ego has fear, and I had to turn the fear over to the higher power or God.

"Seek ye first the Kingdom of God and all things shall be added unto you."

I always tell young advisors, as I tell my kids, "when you do something great, give credit to God." Don't spike the ball in the end zone and do a dance—just put the ball down and go back to the huddle. The small self, or ego, wants to think it is the doer; I know better. God is the doer.

If you have fear, turn it over to God also. It is an illusion. It's the ego, and it's a parasitic, grabbing thing. Today I remember the lesson of *A Course in Miracles*. Nothing real can be threatened. Nothing unreal exists. Therein lies the peace of God.

A great Hall of Fame baseball player once said of future Hall of Famer Derek Jeter of the New York Yankees, "What's great about Jeter is he acts like he has done it before." Jeter obviously has faith. He is a humble superstar, God's greatness on a baseball field.

We will talk more about dissolving the ego and realizing the self in the next chapter.

✻   *"Whether you think you can, or think you can't, you're right."*

— *Henry Ford*

CONTEMPLATION

Consider deeply the road you have travelled, the journey thus far. Can you recall the difficult moments along the path, when it became rocky, perhaps almost impassable? What were the qualities you had to call upon in order to move forward? What virtues were born in you as a result?

Take a few soft, gentle deep breaths and vividly recall your most challenging times and appreciate what came out of them. Can you see the deeper reasons behind it all?

CHAPTER 4

Dissolving the Ego and Realizing the Self

"The sages realized that to understand the mind and make it steady, purity of thought and concentration were necessary. Towards this goal, they prescribed certain spiritual practices. These were broadly classified as Bhakti yoga (yoga of devotion), Karma yoga (yoga of righteous action), and Jnana yoga (yoga of self-discovery)."

—Nisargadatta Maharaj, *Meditations with Sri Nisargadatta Maharaj*, translation by Suresh Mehta and Dinkar Kshirsagar

"I want to sing like birds sing not worrying who is listening or what they think."

—Rumi

It Tried to Prepare Me

*"The clear night sky tried to prepare me for
what it knew would someday happen; it began to
show me ever deeper aspects of its splendor, and
then one evening just directly asked, 'Will you be
able to withstand your own magnificence?'*

*I thought I was just hearing things, until
a spring orchard I was passing my days with
at the height of its glory burst into song, about
our—every human's—destiny to burn with
radiance.*

*Still I felt my ears were playing tricks on me
until the morning came when God tore apart my
chest . . . needing more room to bloom inside.
I began to roll through the streets in ecstasy.
Everyone thought I was crazy.*

*I hope everyone someday knows how blessed
I was. You will."*

—Hafiz

We never completely dissolve the ego because we need ego
to do everyday things like drive a car or go to work. We need at
least some ego, some of that mind portal, in our lives to survive
and function in the world. It's the overemphasis on the personal
that causes problems and can really make people sick and suffer.
The ego is that mind that starts in as soon as we wake up in the
morning.

The renowned sage Sri Nisargadatta Maharaj (1896-1981), in
a very early written work, *Self Knowledge and Self Realization*,
published in 1963, stated, "The ever-awaited first moment was
the moment when I was convinced that I was not an individual
at all. The idea of my individuality had set me burning so far.
The scalding pain was beyond my capacity to endure; but there
is not even a trace of it now, I am no more an individual. There
is nothing to limit my being now. The ever-present anxiety
and the gloom have vanished and now I am all beatitude, pure
knowledge, pure consciousness . . . I am ever free now. I am all

bliss, sans spite, sans fear. This beatific conscious form of mine now knows no bounds. I belong to all and everyone is mine. The 'all' are but my own individuations, and these together go to make up my beatific being . . . Bliss reclines on the bed of bliss. The repose itself has turned into bliss . . . All the characteristics of the Saint naturally spring from his experience [as the nondual Self of all]. As there are no desires left in him, nothing in the world of sense can ever tempt him, he lives in the fearless majesty of Self-realization. He is moved to compassion by the unsuccessful struggle of those tied down to bodily identity and their striving for the satisfaction of their petty interests . . . The Saint who has direct experience of all this is always happy and free from desire. He is convinced that the greatest of the sense experiences is only a momentary affair, impermanence is the very essence of these experiences; hence pain and sorrow, greed and temptation, fear and anxiety can never touch him . . ."

I explained in Chapter 1 that the ego is a separation from God. According to *A Course in Miracles* by Dr. Helen Schucman, this could be the allegory of Adam and Eve, the archetypal human beings who are disobedient, sinful, and prone to suffering, misperceiving themselves as the causal agent. But it's the mind needing to feel that separation, and it's the small self (or the small "I") that is the ego saying, "Mine, mine, mine, me, me, me." This is directly opposed to the true Self or soul, which is part of universal consciousness and is that true, eternal, unchanging beingness divorced of ego. Consider what Jesus said, "It is easier for a camel to go through the eye of a needle than for a rich man to enter into the kingdom of heaven" (Mark 10:25). The eye of the needle parable is the need to die to the self, the small self and its obsession with material considerations. Just carrying the thought of being something more than just the eternal true Self is an illusion.

When we shed the illusions of the world and stand naked in front of our source with humility and love in our hearts, now we have found the true self. Again, we are not our bank accounts, our social status, our affinity groups, our careers, our houses, our cars. I am you and you are me and we are all in it together . . . universal consciousness. As God told Moses when asked, "What is your name?" in Exodus 3.14 of the Torah, the reply was: "I Am that I Am." *Ehyeh aser ehyeh.* These concepts are very hard to adhere to and to digest in one reading. No one, including myself, is saying we are to abandon all material things and meditate all day. However, if we want to experience our birthright—the peace of God that surpasses all worldly thought—then a high degree of discernment is needed. When you look at the wisdom teachings such as Jesus's eye of the needle parable, this is where He was going. The kingdom of peace within, or Heaven, is hard to reach on the inside when we are holding onto ego-driven mindfulness and our illusions of a personal self as the doer of deeds.

Acute sensitivity of awareness of our true inner nature is key. This requires focus. As Jesus said, "Knock and the door shall be opened." Once we get a seed of the truth of ourselves, we begin to transform. Before long, we are on the road to liberation. The candle has been lit.

YIELDING TO THE PRESENCE OF PERFECT LOVE

What did Jesus mean when He said, "I am the way and the truth and the light"? What He is talking about is Christ consciousness. This was not a man talking, but the Spirit of Life talking through a man who had surrendered himself. The Hindus call it Atman, which is "in-dwelling God" and refers to the nonmaterial self that never changes. It is distinct from both the mind and the external body. Buddhists call it "Buddha Nature." When the Buddha became enlightened, he realized that all beings without exception have the same nature and potential for enlightenment. Christians call this the soul. Being saved or saving the soul, according to the Roman Catholic Church and various other Christian teachings, is the surrender to this higher consciousness that is personified by Jesus, our personal savior, and actualized by the power of the Holy Spirit—the electrical cable to God. Another way of putting it is that my sense of self is the plug, Jesus is the socket, the Holy Spirit is the electrical wire, and God is the electricity. The beauty of the Christian model is that Jesus is a personal savior—a socket made of perfect love designed specifically for you.

Through my studies, contemplation, and spiritual practice, I have been able to realize that the idea of nonduality—or being

one with God, as the Hindu Yoga traditions would describe it—
is an experience of the highest of levels of consciousness. Most
would agree that Jesus Christ reached this level of consciousness,
whether one believes He was anointed by God, or that he
simply transcended His humanism into it. After studying other
spiritual wisdom traditions and then restudying the words of
Jesus, I have come to understand He was giving us a blueprint
for transcendence. I don't need to debate anything else. This
transcendence is the potential that everyone has to experience.
Everybody has this Divinity within him or her. We just have to
focus and become aware of it and allow it to fully be. We need to
remove the sheaths of ego that are covering it. To the beautiful
Hindu tradition, this process is called self realization. For them
this is wisdom and truth. True self-awareness is the beginning
of changing the way you see reality. Instead of looking outward
at objects, you can observe that looking. Dr. David R. Hawkins
put it this way: "Realization or enlightenment is the condition
where the sense of self moves from the limited linear material
to the nonlinear infinite and formless.[3] The 'me' moves from the
visible to the invisible. This occurs as a shift of awareness and
identification from perception of form as objective and real to
the realization of the purely subjective as the Ultimate Reality."
Awareness becomes aware of itself.

The beautiful quality of Christian mysticism is that all of
this is an experience of perfect love. There is a tendency on the
spiritual path to intellectualize, but this is a path of yielding to
the abiding presence of eternal love—the holy presence of God.

According to the great Indian sage Ramana Maharshi
(1879–1950), whom Carl Jung referred to as the purest of
India, the whitest spot in a white space, "the only true and
full awareness is awareness of awareness." This is the move
to nonduality. We usually think of experience as dualistic:
good or bad, enjoyable or painful, dull or enriching, desirable
or awful. Even in a spiritual context, we are evaluating how
beneficial, transcendent, calming, or powerful they may be.
Nonduality melts the seeker and the sought, when exhaustively
contemplated, into "at one-ment." This is the Christian origin of

---

3   From Dr. Hawkins book, Reality and Subjectivity, S. 304, 2003

the word "atonement." Buddhism and the Yogic Hindu wisdom are aiming at this incredible understanding. Jesus taught it, but later it was misinterpreted and downplayed by the church in the third century. For example, the Canon Gospels left out Thomas and Mary Magdalene.

Maharshi also said, "Till awareness is awareness of itself, it knows no peace at all. Again, the ego gets in the way. True natural awareness which goes not after alien objects is the heart. Since actionless awareness shines as real being, its joy consists in concentration on itself. Inquiry is making the mind abide firm in the Self till the false ego, illusion's seed, has perished."

This is what Jesus was referring to when He said, "The kingdom of heaven is within you." Self-realization.

On March 13, 1936, a devotee from Bombay asked Ramana Maharshi a question while attending his Ashram: "Do I keep my mind blank without thoughts arising so that God might show himself in his true being?"

Maharshi answered: "The essence of mind is only awareness or consciousness. However, when the ego dominates, it functions as the reasoning, thinking, or sensing faculty. The cosmic mind, not being limited by the ego, has nothing separate from itself and is, therefore, only aware. That is what the Bible means by 'I Am that I Am.' The ego-ridden mind has its strength sapped and is too weak to resist the torturing thoughts. The egoless mind is happy in deep, dreamless sleep. Clearly therefore, bliss and misery are only modes of mind; but the weak mode is not easily interchangeable with the strong mode. Activity is weakness and consequently miserable; passivity is strength and therefore not utilized. The cosmic mind, manifesting in some rare being is able to effect the linkage in others of the individual (weak) mind with the universal (strong) mind of the inner recess. Such a rare being is called the Guru or God in manifestation."

In my spiritual experience, Jesus would be an example of such a rare being that Maharshi was referring to in the above quote.

Recall in John 8:58, Jesus said to them, "Truly, truly, I say to you, before Abraham was born, I am."

HOW TO DISSOLVE THE EGO AND
REALIZE THE SELF

According to the teachings of Bhagavan Sri Ramana Maharshi, "The axe to cut down the ego is through Self enquiry Who am I." (Nan Yar)

Jnana yoga (yoga of self-discovery): This is the yoga of wisdom and knowledge and requires great strength of will and intellect. The mind is used to inquire into its own nature to transcend its identity with its thoughts and ego. This is a process of asking yourself a series of questions of "Who are you?", "Who am I?" and one by one answering, "I am not this," "I am not that," until what you are left with is only pure awareness. This is one of the fastest ways to sense the sheaths covering the true self, eliminate the awareness of the ego, and move toward Self-Realization. Bhakti yoga (yoga of devotion) to God is another powerful way to tear down the Ego and move toward Self-Realization. I have found these Yoga practices combined with Karma Yoga (yoga of righteous action/ helping others and living a virtuous life) to be a potent way of supercharging my spiritual practice, growing closer to God and liberating my soul.

The mind is drawn in by the senses (touch, feel, smell, sight, and taste), and we're in this realm here on earth, and we feel like this is it—everything is so real, pressing and important—but again, the true nature of reality is that it's not everything.

We're really here for a reason, and that reason is to create love and to be compassionate. And to grow spiritually. We are here to realize the Self and rediscover the soul. When we reach a certain point, we aspire that even the seeker cannot be found. This is atonement.

When we can stand back and observe the thoughts and impressions that flow through the mind and become the witness to them and not be attached to them, we shine forth as the timeless infinite awareness. The Self, which is our true being or the soul, is that awareness. Instead of looking outward at objects, we observe that looking. We sense that we are connecting to the source of all existence, melting into one with the present moment, which is infinite consciousness, or God. Some may call it the supreme state. I have come to understand this to be Christ consciousness.

My heart tells me to learn the truth of things directly from my *self*. In other words, from the heart, the higher intuition and understanding of the spirit, as opposed to the sensory interpretation from the attachment of the *ego* mind to mental chatter, physical senses, and the polarized (good or bad) stimulation of the material world.

When I am the witness to my consciousness and aware of awareness, I feel like I am one with the world and one with divinity. I can sense the truth of Jesus's teachings. This is atonement. My personality falls away, and even the so-called "seeker" in me drops away. I feel an alignment with all, and my ego and personality disappear. This is a rare state for me to be in; however, just the taste of this state of being and its bliss have given me a strong faith and knowingness in God and of the truth of the Wisdom teachings that I cover in this book.

As a matter of fact, once this bliss is experienced, even if just for a moment, our perception of life is never the same.

Much of what the ego generates in thought and comparisons and judgments are mere illusions. Yet, the paradox is that one needs to be careful of the karma that is created. For as Jesus said, "What we sow, we reap." We create our own reality, whether heaven or hell.

At the end of the day, many of us have challenges because we're in the world every day—we have to live in the world, work in it—so it's not easy to always have this level of consciousness. What is important is to aspire to raise your level of consciousness in all your affairs and dealings, to have awareness and the willingness to grow. The Eastern philosophies call this creating "Good Karma." Karma is the idea of cause and effect. We all can sense the reality of causing our realities by our deeds, words, and actions. This would also explain the idea and concept of having "Bad Karma." Again, we reap what we sow.

I have even seen business consultants using this concept, as awareness of its truth begins to permeate. I believe we can maintain this higher level of consciousness and still function in the business world and the world in general by maintaining an attitude of service to others. In the *Bhagavad Gita*, Krishna said, "Do your duties but don't attach yourself to the results." In other words, we give our best efforts in all our affairs, but we don't attach our ego to the results. We are not the ultimate doer. We are agents of God.

Don't attach yourself to the results you get, and when you do well, know that you are not the doer. God is acting through you. God is the doer in everything. Have gratitude for God's grace. I know from personal experience how little power I had as a young man running on my own ego, running on my own illusions of what life was supposed to mean, and who I thought I was. At one point, I felt as though I had been hit on the head by a two-by-four. I was actually hit over the head by an automobile, a Buick, to be exact. In this surrendering from my weakest point, I was given strength from this higher power that is beyond description, which I have grown to understand is all powerful, omnipresent, omnipotent, and omniscient. What is interesting is that it is also that still awareness or beingness that is exactly this higher Self Maharshi is referring to. Again, it may be called different things such as Christ consciousness or Buddha nature or Atman, but it is inside all of us, eternal and divine. As I went further along the path, I realized it wasn't just about loving myself, loving my family, and loving my own children. It was about loving everyone and everyone's children. Loving your own family isn't enough—you have to love everyone.

Jesus said this in Matthew 5:46-48, "If you love those who love you, what reward will you get? Are not even the tax collectors doing that? And if you greet only your own people, what are you doing more than others? Do not even pagans do that? Be perfect, therefore, as your heavenly Father is perfect."

But it's not like you have to because you are forcing yourself to, white-knuckling; it becomes natural to you when you see reality from its true nature. It's a different level of consciousness. And when you awaken to it, it's not like you have to battle to be nice and to love; it's easy because your mind is transformed. It's a different playing field. It also becomes natural to say you're sorry when you fail or make a mistake. We forgive ourselves as we are forgiven and as we forgive others. Holding onto guilt and resentments is like holding onto clouds; they are illusions and not real.

Luke 11:1-13
Jesus's Teaching on Prayer

One day Jesus was praying in a certain place. When he finished, one of his disciples said to him, "Lord, teach us to pray, just as John taught his disciples."

He said to them, "When you pray, say:

'Father, hallowed be your name, your kingdom come.

Give us each day our daily bread.

Forgive us our sins, for we also forgive everyone who sins against us.

And lead us not into temptation.'

Then Jesus said to them, "Suppose you have a friend, and you go to him at midnight and say, 'Friend, lend me three loaves of bread;

a friend of mine on a journey has come to me, and I have no food to offer him.'

And suppose the one inside answers, 'Don't bother me. The door is already locked, and my children and I are in bed. I can't get up and give you anything.'

I tell you, even though he will not get up and give you the bread because of friendship, yet because of your shameless audacity he will surely get up and give you as much as you need.

So I say to you: Ask and it will be given to you; seek and you will find; knock and the door will be opened to you.

For everyone who asks receives; the one who seeks finds; and to the one who knocks, the door will be opened."

Again, that was the message of Christ the Jesus of the East, whose message is not quite the same as the Jesus of the Western traditions. With the Eastern Wisdom Jesus, He emerges as a teacher of the transformation of consciousness, similar to Buddha's Dhammapada, and to Krishna's Bhagavad Gita.

ANOTHER VIEW OF JESUS'S MESSAGE

Metanoia. What does it mean? According to Cynthia Bourgeault, "It is the escape from the orbit of the ego, the operating system which, by virtue of its own internal handwriting, is always going to see the world in terms of polarized opposites and move instead into the nondual knowingness of the heart that can see and live from the perspective of wholeness." The following description is taken from Chapter 4 in her beautiful book, *The Wisdom Jesus: Transforming Heart and Mind—A New Perspective on Christ and His Message.* She discusses the Beatitudes and what they mean. For example, "Blessed are the pure of heart for they will see God" may well be the most important of all the Beatitudes—from the perspective of wisdom, it certainly is—but what is "pure of heart"?

According to Bourgeault, "This is another of those concepts we have distorted in our very morale-oriented Christianity of the West. For most people, purity of heart would almost certainly mean being virtuous, particularly in the sexual arena. It would be roughly synonymous with chastity, perhaps even celibacy, but in wisdom teaching purity means singleness and the proper translation of this beatitude is really, 'Blessed are those whose heart is not divided or whose heart is a unified whole.'"

Bourgeault mentions in Chapter 2 of her book that "Ihidaya is the word in the Aramaic language given to Jesus by his immediate followers and is one of the earliest titles given to Him." Ihidaya means the Single One, or the Unified One. In context, she continues, "It speaks unmistakably of this state of inner oneness; it's the fully realized human being, the enlightened master of Eastern tradition." Farther in her book Bourgeault points out, "This enlightenment takes place primarily within the heart . . . when your heart becomes single, that is when it desires one thing only, when it can live in perfect alignment with that resonant field of mutual yearning that we call the Righteousness of God. Then you see God. But this does not mean you see God as an object because that would be the ego operating system, but instead you see through the eyes of nonduality . . . God is the 'seeing' itself."

This is the Yogi of the East. Again, in Jesus's own words, "The kingdom of heaven is within you."

We can see from Bourgeault's Jesus the congruency with all the other wisdom teachers, for instance, Krishna and the Yogi traditions, as well as the Buddha and his teachings on Enlightenment. When the great Tao of ancient Chinese wisdom teachings is examined, it, too, resonates this nonduality. What is also interesting is that Bourgeault, aside from being a great spiritual author and mystic, is also an Episcopal priest.

> *"There is a sun in every person, the you we call companion."*
>
> —*Rumi*

CONTEMPLATION

Close your eyes, and take a few soft, gentle deep breaths. Drop into the awareness of your heart. Feel your heart like an empty cup. Simply breathe, and allow that cup to be filled by the Presence of Life. Do not interfere with your thoughts. Simply allow your heart to be filled. Smile, and gently breathe. Offer your heart cup, the Holy Grail of your being, to the Spirit of Life. Do this with tender, humble love. Allow yourself to be filled until your cup runneth over.

CHAPTER 5

Awakening to the True Nature of Reality

"*Jesus saw infants being suckled. He said to His disciples, 'These infants being suckled are like those who enter the Kingdom.' They said to Him, 'Shall we then, as children, enter the Kingdom?' Jesus said to them, 'When you make the two one, and when you make the inside like the outside and the outside like the inside, and the above like the below, and when you make the male and the female one and the same, so that the male not be male nor the female female; and when you fashion eyes in the place of an eye, and a hand in place of a hand, and a foot in place of a foot, and a likeness in place of a likeness; then will you enter [the Kingdom].'*"

—*Excerpt From: Didymos Judas Thomas, "The Gospel of Thomas"*

This quotation has a ring to it very similar to Buddhist and Hindu teachings of abandonment of the material. Thomas actually is saying that children are closer to enlightenment (so to speak) than adults are.

In my opinion, this could be because Jesus realizes that babies have not yet formed or psychologically developed an attachment to an individual ego consciousness and the perception of being an individual causal agent. They have not yet perceived themselves as an independent Jiva, or the doer of deeds. They have not yet developed into the individual that speaks from the standpoint of me, mine, or I. In essence, they have not yet learned duality.

Jesus is giving an incredible insight into nonduality.

Nondualism, also called "nonduality," means not two, and it points to the idea that the universe and all its multiplicity are ultimately expressions or appearances of one essential reality. It is a term and concept used to define various strands of religious and spiritual thought. It is found in a variety of Asian religious traditions and modern Western spirituality, but with a variety of meanings and uses.

> *"There is no peace without love and no love without peace."*
> —*A Course in Miracles*

My studies of the Eastern philosophies and religions have strengthened my faith in the Western Jesus tradition I grew up with. Yet it also gave me respect for all the great traditions of spiritual universal curriculums. It was due to my study of Buddhism and Hinduism that I really came to understand the transformative message of Jesus.

> *"The light of the body is the eye: if therefore thine eye be single, thy whole body shall be full of light."*
> —*Matthew 6:22*

This is an example of an Eastern teaching by Jesus similar to Buddhism and Hinduism. Its tremendous insight goes far beyond the obvious. The eye pertains to inner consciousness, because everything is inner consciousness. Many believe Jesus was referring to the Ajna chakra.

Ajna (Sanskrit: IAST Ājñā, English: "command") or third eye chakra is the sixth primary chakra, according to Hindu traditions. The Ajna chakra is positioned in the brain, directly behind the eyebrow center. Its activation site is at the eyebrow region in the position of the third eye.

It's as if Jesus was saying that if the only thing we see is Oneness, our eye is single, and we are full of light and see things the way God sees them.

> *"If I do not get established in wisdom now, when shall another opportunity arise? For, indulgence in sense-pleasure poisons the mind in such a way that its effects last several lifetimes. Only the man of self-knowledge is free from this. Therefore, O sage, I pray to thee: instruct me in such a way that I may forever be free from anguish, fear, and distress. With the light of your instruction, destroy the darkness of ignorance in my heart."*
>
> *—Vasistha's Yoga, by Swami Venkatesananda*

Have you ever wondered about the common threads of all the world's great wisdom traditions? Have you ever wondered what we are doing here and why we are here? Notice the beauty and similarities between the Tao Te Ching (using Stephen Mitchell's translation) and the Holy Bible.

Tao Te Ching

Do you want to improve the world?

I don't think it can be done.

The world is sacred.

It can't be improved.

If you tamper with it, you'll ruin it.

If you treat it like an object, you'll lose it.

There is a time for being ahead,

a time for being behind;

a time for being in motion,

a time for being at rest;

a time for being vigorous,

a time for being exhausted;

a time for being safe,

a time for being in danger.

The Master sees things as they are,

without trying to control them.

She lets them go their own way,

and resides at the center of the circle.

—*Lao-tzu,* Tao Te Ching 29, *translation by
Stephen Mitchell*

Holy Bible
Ecclesiastes 3 New International Version (NIV)
A Time for Everything

There is a time for everything,

and a season for every activity under the heavens:

a time to be born and a time to die,

a time to plant and a time to uproot,

a time to kill and a time to heal,

a time to tear down and a time to build,

a time to weep and a time to laugh,

a time to mourn and a time to dance,

a time to scatter stones and a time to gather them,

a time to embrace and a time to refrain from embracing,

a time to search and a time to give up,

a time to keep and a time to throw away,

a time to tear and a time to mend,

a time to be silent and a time to speak,

a time to love and a time to hate,

a time for war and a time for peace.

This Bible passage is also a beautiful song from the 1960s called "Turn, Turn, Turn," written by Pete Seeger and covered by Judy Collins and The Byrds. Can you remember the powerful effect that this song had on you when you sat with its beautiful lyrics and truth?

THE TRUE NATURE OF REALITY

Most of us are spiritually lost; we are like lost sheep trying to have that fellowship and that love with others, yet find it difficult to escape the Egoic mind and its gravitational pulls. I know I felt this way most of my early life. In the Gospel of Thomas, Jesus talked about taming the wild animal energy within oneself as "devouring the lion because, otherwise, the lion will devour us." This is a very interesting Gospel that was not part of the Canonical Gospels. This Gospel was buried in the early days of Christianity sometime in the early 3rd or 4th century and then rediscovered by a farmer in the Egyptian desert in 1945. It is famous for its reference to Jesus saying, "The Kingdom of heaven is within you." It appears to me that Jesus was aware of something very true about life here on earth and life after we die. It's as if He understood the true nature of reality, similar to the message of Buddha and the great Hindu yoga sutras.

We have to deal with our sense of fear and scarcity that emerges out of our Egoic operating system. It's almost like we have amnesia due to our Egoic experience from the five senses.

As I mentioned in the previous chapter, by understanding that compassion and love really flow naturally when we see the true nature of reality, we won't be or feel lost anymore once we cross this threshold of awareness. As we become more compassionate, loving, and forgiving and release our addiction to positionality/judgment, we begin to experience life from a deeper, more real perspective. Obviously, Jesus saw this. He was referred to by his disciples as the Ihidaya, or single one. He became one with God. He became the Christ.

The good news is that you and I can awaken to this mental, physical, emotional, and spiritual transformation as well. It's almost as if we have a full body addiction to the ego mind in this realm.

So what is the true nature of reality? In one of his most beautiful insights, contemporary Christian mystic Thomas Merton wrote, "At the center of our being is a point of nothingness which is untouched by sin and illusion, a point of pure truth, a spark which belongs entirely to God." In Buddhism it is called dharma (in Sanskrit). This word, which is foundational to the conceptual framework of the Indian religions, refers to the system of natural laws that constitute the natural order of things. The teaching of the Buddha is that people can come out of their condition of suffering (dukkha), and this process involves developing an awareness of reality (mindfulness). Dharma is, therefore, reality as it is. One of the most discussed themes in Buddhism is that of the emptiness (sunyata) of form (matter), an important corollary of the transient and conditioned nature of phenomena. Reality is seen ultimately, in Buddhism, as a form of projection resulting from the fruition of Karmic seeds.

It was very helpful to me and my spiritual development to understand this, as opposed to continuing to fall for the illusions of the Egoic mind.

We drop the story of our ego and instead let ourselves work from our hearts and let that vibrate out to others. As you may know, everything is energy and vibration, and when we are vibrating at a different frequency, we have a different voice.

Humility is knowing the true nature of reality and understanding that it's not just desires and wants, because we will never be able to fill that wanting—it's insatiable. It's an unfillable well. It's somewhat like the person who keeps building piles and piles and piles of money—what's he going to do someday? He will roll over and die. Jesus would have said he was already dead and needs to be reborn into spirit. It's similar to Charles Dickens' famous *A Christmas Carol* and the character of Scrooge, who on the Christmas morning after his nightmare truly awakened.

The ego of the insatiable desire for wealth will drive you to a spiritual death, chasing something that's an illusion. I'm not saying you shouldn't do your best. As the Hindus believe—and as the Bhagavad Gita and Krishna's message point to—you do your best, serve, but don't attach yourself to the results so tightly. It's a matter of humility in our hearts, and that's the projection we bring from the soul. The heart is the Holy Grail, and you have to offer it up. It's the path of the sacred heart of Jesus. It's a knowingness. It's a modern scientific fact we can change our DNA, our blood, our actual spirit by changing what we say in our minds and in our hearts. We're changing it from the heart, from the inside out. Most of us never can dissolve it completely. We are looking for progress, not perfection.

Eventually, we reach a point somewhere down the road where words even drop away; everything is going to drop away, and in the spiritual realm when we become one with that universal consciousness (yogi) or the divine spirit, at that point words are not even spoken, they are not needed. We think we can add one plus one to equal two. How everything should just add up. But we don't understand the universal consciousness of God to a point where we can really be on that level. We can't understand the timelessness and omniscience of God. We do, however, need to keep developing our faith and our awareness by our spiritual practices and start to see through the eyes of the Christ.

FORGIVENESS

There is an ancestral prayer from the ancient Hawaiian culture called *ho'oponopono* that literally means "the restoration of harmony or righteousness through forgiveness." The actual prayer is very long, but the key core essence is, "I am sorry, please forgive me, thank you, I love you." It is extremely effective in dissolving the negativity that prevents us from enjoying the underlying peace of pure consciousness.

Forgiveness is the key to happiness, and the word originally meant to both give and receive—"to give for." Keeping with the original meaning, we can see that the inner reward for forgiveness is the exchange of life . . . the give and take between our soul and the universe. Forgiveness is the key. It's the answer. In *A Course in Miracles*, "The unforgiving mind sees no mistakes, only sins," but it's also a very, very important part of my own experience. I had to forgive myself over the years and learn not to be "frozen" in terms of how I reacted when taking that test in college, and to not be frozen when trying to forgive others. If you hate others, you hate yourself. If you love others, you love yourself. This is a natural law and the law of karma.

One of the ironies I always think about in contemporary times is when President Richard Nixon resigned from the White House. I always felt compassion for Nixon because he was very Shakespearean in terms of his drama: wanting to be President so badly, then becoming President, and because of his own fears and anger toward those who disliked him, he lost the White House. The irony is what he had said to his staff and his cabinet, as he was looking at them in tears before getting ready to fly off in the presidential helicopter for the last time. He warned them, "Remember, when people hate you, you don't hate them back because when you do, all you do is hurt yourself." It seems as though by reacting to disharmony, we add to disharmony. If we don't react to it or resist it, it dissolves on its own and does not grow. The teaching of Christ to "resist not evil" is a hint to not respond to disharmony.

A Hawaiian doctor became a teacher of clearing disharmony in a psychiatric maximum-security prison, to which he was recruited in 1983. No one wanted to work at the prison because it was too dangerous, and mostly populated by violent murderers and very sick people. The staff would call in sick, and the paint on the walls was cracking. The place was a negative, dark place.

By praying for the prisoners without even meeting the inmates and by praying the *ho'oponopono* prayer over their files, Dr. Hew Len helped heal the population in the hospital to a point where, thankfully, the prison was closed. His process has been highly studied as a verification of the great wisdom teachings and virtues of forgiveness that we have been discussing. It is the prayer of practicing forgiveness and saying, "I am sorry, please forgive me, thank you, I love you" that clears the mind and leaves room for God's inspiration. We need to say this to those who have left us—parents, ancestors, grandparents—and for the people who are in our life today. We need to heal the disharmony.

LOVE AND COMPASSION

Nothing works like love and compassion. They raise the level of your vibration to the public and to the people you are working with. Notre Dame coach and sportscaster Lou Holtz always said, "I can't hear what you are saying until I know you care."

A client of mine came in recently, and we were looking at pictures of the two of us standing next to each other when we were playing PONY league baseball at age 13. I sat with him for a couple of hours, talking about his life and his future. He was worried about his financial affairs. I consoled and counseled him. After I gathered all the information we needed to complete and update his written investment plan, I said, in so many words, "We're going to take care of you, we're going to love you, we're going to care for you, we're going to plan for you, we're going to follow the wealth protection process and follow Modern Portfolio Theory." I also told him, "We're going to plan for your desired lifestyle and retirement, do a budget, look at what you're spending, what are your Social Security benefits, and anything else that is coming in. Then we'll take a look at your risk tolerance and talk about what can happen in bear markets." This was all very helpful to him.

In the upcoming chapters I will explain everything and go into greater detail about the investment process, because this all leads to the importance of having an investment process, which is the foundation for all that we do.

But the point is, we need to do this from the heart, which is why I am explaining in much of the first part of this book about love, heart, universal consciousness, peace, and harmony. We can do everything based on what textbooks recommend as the best way to manage and allocate money, but in reality we have to rely on the verdict of history, and then we have to trust in God if we want to really be at peace with our insecurities about money and our lives. I always think about the monks; this is where I have personally obtained so much freedom. I don't need much for myself. Of course, I don't want my family to suffer, and they don't because I can provide for them. However, I know that I could be happy just having good food, being warm, and having some spiritual books to read and enlighten me.

Your reality is really based on your associations and what you've been taught, what you've learned, and what you've inherited in the mind. This is why, when you change the nature of your reality, you stop the fears, attachments, judgments, comparing, and everything that goes with the Egoic mind. Then you go to silent peace, and you fill it with the heart and the knowledge of the grace of God and start to focus on filling the space with inspiration. That's exactly what Buddhism is—that's exactly what true wisdom Christianity is, and it's exactly what being unified with God and Hinduism is.

When you awaken to the true nature of reality, you're starting over, you're changing and clearing your mind, and now you are out there and you see the bird. Now you see the sun hitting the tree and the bird lifting off. It's such peace; you've got a peace beyond understanding. It's dying to the small self and being reborn. It's Maharshi's Self-Awareness, Self-Realization. Again, sometimes we have to seek a little bit more to get there, or we have to run into some dead ends, surrender, get hit on the head with a two-by-four or a Buick, whatever it takes.

You see, nothing really is, as Shakespeare said, but what we think it is. "I think, therefore I am," Descartes said, but he was not right. Sartre came along years later and rightly pointed out, "There is an awareness beyond the thinker."

The Eastern traditions have known this for years and have long believed this awareness is the beginning of Self-Realization and the path to freedom and real peace.

The Master (Jesus) clearly taught this in the Gospels.

Jesus was once asked when the kingdom of God would come. The kingdom of God, Jesus replied, is not something people will be able to see and point to. Then came these striking words: "Neither shall they say, Lo here! or, lo there! for behold, the kingdom of God is within you." (Luke 17:21).

With these words, Jesus gave voice to a teaching that is universal and timeless. Look into every great religious, spiritual, and wisdom tradition, and we find the same precept—that life's ultimate truth, its ultimate treasure, lies within us. "The kingdom of heaven is within you." But you first must die to the small self, the ego, before you enter the kingdom.

Unbroken Chain

> *"November and more as I wait for the score*
> *They're telling me forgiveness is the key to every door*
> *A slow winter day, a night like forever*
> *Sink like a stone, float like a feather."*[4]

CONTEMPLATION

Consider deeply anyone and anything you need to forgive in your life. How is hanging onto grievances, judgment, and old hurts serving you today? Go deep within yourself. Feel that empty cup of your heart again and say the *ho'oponopono* prayer: I am sorry. Please forgive me. Thank you. I love you.

You are not forgiving them because you condone what they have done; instead, you are forgiving them to lighten your own load. Forgive everyone, forgive everything, and most of all, forgive yourself. How does taking full responsibility for everything in your life make you feel? How does letting go of ego-victim consciousness feel? Take a few soft, gentle deep breaths, and go deep with this. I am sorry. Please forgive me. I love you. Thank you. Thank you. Thank you.

---

4   See permission for "Unbroken Chain" lyrics in Resources and Permissions section of the book.

CHAPTER 6

The Wanting Mind

"The happiness of one's heart alone cannot satisfy the soul. One must try to include as necessary to one's own happiness the happiness of others."

—*Paramahansa Yogananda*

The "wanting mind" is the craving referred to in different Buddhist traditions as a force that—whether it is money, love, a higher investment return, a better world, or anything else we are searching for—is the part of our mind that tells us things need to change in order for us to be happy. The problem with this mindset is that it causes suffering.

The craving exists because of our belief that what we have right now can't possibly be good enough. It constantly takes us out of the present moment to focus on tomorrow, next week, next year, five years from now, and on and on. Unless we really look into it and see the hidden workings of this state of mind, we remain a slave to it, and we spend an entire lifetime chasing images to find peace as opposed to finding peace in the present moment. It is like the idea of being a passenger on a train as it goes by different stations, and we believe when we reach the next station, we will be happy. So we get to the next station, but we are not happy. We continue on, going to many stations looking for happiness, but we never reach the destination of happiness because we are always putting something else in front of us before we allow ourselves to be content. It's the illusion of always reaching for the brass ring, but not being able to grasp it. There never seems to be enough, but when we begin to understand how the mind is wired to avoid pain and when we see through it clearly, we begin to take it less personally. Why is it that we are never content in the present moment?

When John D. Rockefeller was asked how much is enough, he replied, "Just a little bit more." Ben Franklin said, "Wealth is not his that has it, but his that enjoys it." And Samuel Johnson said, "Every man is rich or poor according to the proportion between his desires and his enjoyments." The idea is that if your wishes align with your purse, the amount of money in it doesn't much matter.

As mentioned earlier, from the Buddhist teachings we learn that desire causes suffering. I was inspired by the Trappist monks like Thomas Merton, and the Buddhist monks that I read about—whether it was the Catholic tradition or the Buddhist tradition. They seem to live in the present moment and be at peace. This is not to say that we don't try to do our best and build wealth and savings for security and for our family's future. We can still plan properly for our children's education and our retirements —and at the same time not waste our precious moments on this earth stuck in the illusion of worry and fear—if we know how. It really comes back to the concept of nonattachment and the message of the *Bhagavad Gita* and Buddha and the wisdom of Jesus. We do our best, we plan, but we don't attach ourselves to the result. Living one day at a time to its fullest is the answer.

One of the first things we do in the planning process is look at the monthly and annual spending budgets. Believe me when I tell you we need to prioritize our discretionary spending.

Many young families get caught up in the peer pressure of society and their social groups' spending patterns. Unfortunately, the media and some of the commercials we and our children are exposed to reinforce the wrong message. What comes to mind is a car commercial showing a family getting into their brand new car, as the family next door looks on with a sad and jealous look of embarrassment. Many take this media message for real. It is not. It is an illusion. What is sad is the spirit behind it. We need to make good decisions and prioritize our spending early in our family formations, and plan for our security and financial liberation.

WHAT DO WE REALLY NEED?

What we need to realize about the ego and the mind is that it is always going to tell us we need certain things that, in many cases, we don't really need. When we reach that real peace beyond understanding, that peace is very, very deep, but it takes practice to reach that level. The idea of being without all of those other things we think we need can be scary at first. Until we retrain the mind, that is. Then the peaceful element of just being takes over from the restless, wanting mind. But when society tells us what we need, and we have our children who want to do everything the other kids are doing (whether it is a sport, a dance, a video game, an iPhone, wearing Ugg boots, or other things and activities), and the media screams at us with advertisements for products we don't really need, it all adds fuel to the fire of the natural desires we have as humans. Much of the wanting relates back to the ego and its insatiable appetite. And ultimately, it doesn't allow us to be happy.

There is no question that we have legitimate concerns such as having food or shelter. That is what Jesus spoke of when He said to not worry about tomorrow, that the Father is going to take care of us. He told the parable about the lilies and the birds: "Therefore I tell you, do not be anxious about your life, what you will eat, or what you will drink, nor about your body, what you will put on. Is not life more than food, and the body more than clothing? Look at the birds of the air: they neither sow nor reap nor gather into barns, and yet your heavenly Father feeds them. Are you not of more value than they? And why are you anxious about clothing? Consider the lilies of the field, how they grow:

they neither toil nor spin, yet I tell you, even Solomon in all his glory was not arrayed like one of these."

If this sounds old-fashioned or even like a Holy Roller espousing religious rhetoric, I understand. I have felt this way myself in the past. But in truth it is real wisdom, plain and simple. Take a few seconds to really think about its wisdom for a moment before moving on.

There is no question that some of our actions are simply done out of fear, which is, by the way, a parasite. Fear is a symptom of the ego, and the ego is a parasite; it needs to be fed. From a spiritual standpoint fear is not real. Some have described FEAR as the acronym of false evidence appearing real. Have you ever been paralyzed by fear? I know I have. We only have the present moment, so we need to do our jobs to earn a living, for example, but the reality is that we only have the present. It's the mind acting up again. The heart, on the other hand, is really where truth is. When we live in our mind, we are always going to have these desires and fears. The mind is predominantly self-concerned, and in some cases it could be grandiose, usually requiring more financial resources than you can expect to have. Sometimes it also has a childlike urgency attached to it. It's comparative and competitive, and you have desires that feel insatiable, and as soon as one desire is satiated, the mind is onto a new one. Again, I raise my hand to the question of "Have you ever felt this way?"

The heartfelt goal, on the other hand, is realistic and achievable and would have patience attached to it as well. This is what we are talking about here and what really matters.

Trappist monk Thomas Merton said, "Truth is formed in silence, work, and suffering. We talk of God when He has gone far from us. We are far from Him, and His nearness remains to accuse us. We live as if God existed for our sakes, figuring that we exist for Him. We use grace as if it were matter handed over to form according to our pleasure. We use the truth of God as material for the fabrication of idols. We forget that we are the matter and His grace is the form imposed upon us by His wisdom. Does the clay understand the work of the potter? Does it not allow itself to be formed into a vessel of election? This is formed in silence and work and suffering with which we become true. But we interfere with God's work by talking too much about ourselves, even telling

Him what we ought to do, advising Him how to make us perfect, and listening for His voice to answer us with approval. We soon grow impatient and turn aside from the silence that disturbs us, the silence in which His work can best be done, and we invent the answer and the approval, which will never come. Silence then is the adoration of His truth. Work is the expression of our humility, and suffering is born of the love that seeks one thing alone that God's will be done." —November 12, 1952

Merton may be the most prominent Christian writer of the 20th century. He was a mystic writer, and he received a little pushback from traditional Catholics because he was close with men of all faiths and his writings reflected it. He lived alone in a little shed at the Abbey of Gethsemani in Kentucky and wrote many books, including his autobiography, the best-selling *The Seven Storey Mountain*. He was in Thailand visiting the Dalai Lama just weeks before he died in 1968. He was also very good friends with the Vietnamese Zen Buddhist monk and author Thích Nhất Hạnh, who is currently 91 years of age (born in 1926). Merton was once an atheist and became a Catholic priest after attending Oxford. He became a priest after going through what he called his spiritual experience. The title of his autobiography is taken from Dante's *Inferno*, which is the classic 13th century poet's story of climbing the Seven Deadly Sins and rising out of hell to purgatory and finally up to heaven. Musician Bob Dylan referred to Dante in his classic song "Tangled Up in Blue."

GETTING THE MESSAGE ACROSS ABOUT MONEY

In the investment world we explain that we must not look at financial planning simply from the standpoint of "Well, I really need to live on this amount of money each year, and I will be miserable if I can't." If we can go in and look at the source and say, "Here are the necessities, the essential items, and these are the things we need to live comfortably. These other things that we think we need, although they would be nice, they're really not the source of happiness in our life." Tough decisions are sometimes needed. The true liberation and freedom comes from making those decisions from the true self, the source of truth within, as opposed to the pull from the Egoic mind.

Please know I have experienced these tough conversations in my own life with my dear clients and with family members. The point I am trying to convey is that the best things in life are priceless and free. A beautiful sunny day walking the dog by the river, watching birds and animals, hugging our children, helping a friend feel better about some misunderstanding or problem, and loving others.

The list of simple pleasures can go on and on. The key is getting in touch with our truth within and seeing the outside world for its beauty, rather than how our ego can be satisfied.

If we are able to eliminate some of these things that aren't essential in our lives and start to live within our means, then we can do the planning much more cohesively and realistically. What we really do need and what we think we need are entirely different, and usually we are not really thinking consciously about these things. Most of us are affected by how we were brought up with money, and some of us were affected by scarcity. I used to have an issue with it, and I worked through it because it was a deeply rooted association from my current life as well as my genetics. I think I'm getting more comfortable with the scarcity issue. I believe it's just this fear that keeps us paralyzed, thinking that if we make a mistake, it might adversely affect our future. I always worried more about my own humiliation in the eyes of my children. Again, a lot of this springs from my culture and the societal stigma of success versus so-called failure. We are also paralyzed by the past. We all have a horror story about the past of something we have seen, someone who had lost it all, or even just the stories of the Great Depression. We need to look within and ask ourselves questions to understand how much of our story is real versus how much is just what we've had "put on us." Then we have to go further and ask what is even real about any of it.

I think many of us suffer to an extreme over money. It's a matter of really working on that aspect of our life, not so much that we have to keep making more and more money, but that we should begin looking at the source of the suffering, which is the desire. And the illusions of what people think about us. I know that is very different for many people to even hear that concept, but this is the transformative message of Jesus, it's the transformative message of Buddha, and it's the transformative consciousness from the Hindus. It's all the same author and truth, but it comes down to looking at our real personality versus our ego/mind. You might not even say the "real personality;" you might just say this "insatiable ego versus finding the true self within." Illusions of the mind versus the truth that is within everyone. In reality, we are okay, we're going to be okay.

Let's look at the Vietnamese migrant workers who save at a rate of 30%. Their income is drastically lower than many of ours, and they live on an average of less than $4 a day. They save 30% of their income. I don't think they are going to bed hungry; I think they are warm at night, and they have some peace. Many studies have found that the levels of happiness are not higher in more affluent cultures. In many cases, they are lower. But it doesn't have to be so. You can still be happy if you are wealthy. The answer is to develop detachment from association with the wealth as being who you really are.

As far as preparing for retirement, you really need to save, to budget, and to eliminate as many things as you can that are nonessential. You have to do a soul-search to see what is really essential in your life. I'm not talking about giving up something you spend money on that is your passion. What I mean by nonessentials is, for example, I realized at one point I was paying for quite a few TV channels on cable that I never watched. We have to look at where we spend our money every month. That is very important to building future security—the saving, the budgeting, and knowing where you are spending your money.

What good is it to make a lot of money if you are never happy? And what good is it to make just a little bit of money and not be happy? It's about trying to find peace in the moment. If we see the true nature of reality, which we talked about in earlier chapters, and we see how it relates to the present, then even if we have a life-threatening illness, we are still alive, we are living in the present moment, and we are eternal spirits.

Even beyond that is the issue of getting back to the reality behind our existence—living and breathing and sitting and praying and meditating, loving God with all of our heart, mind, soul, and strength. And loving our neighbor as ourselves. We need to get our minds quiet and get ourselves out of the tapes that are constantly running in our heads. Most of them are fearful tapes, especially if we start to think about the future in the sense that we're not going to have enough to live on.

I am a proponent of planning, planning, planning, of course, but at the same time the peace that I have found in my own life after working on it for a long time made me realize it is just a matter of letting go of the world as we know it. And letting go of all of the things outside of ourselves that we think are so real and pressing. We have to look inside for that peace and remember the words of *A Course in Miracles*, "Nothing real can be threatened, nothing unreal exists, therein lies the peace of God. This is the peace that is beyond all understanding!"

As Rumi says in *The Masnavi*, "Man is a captive on earth. His body and his mind are his prison bars. And the soul is unconsciously craving to experience once again the freedom that originally belonged to it."

Comes a Time

> *"Comes a time when the blind man takes your hand, says*
> *'Don't you see?*
> *Gotta make it somehow on the dreams you still believe.'*
> *Don't give it up, you got an empty cup only love can fill,*
> *only love can fill."*[5]

CONTEMPLATION

Consider deeply where your happiness truly lies. What are the things that bring you genuine happiness? Hold those things in your mind's eye. Take a few soft, gentle, deep breaths and fill your heart's cup with the feelings of that truth. Make a short list of these things, circumstances, and people and then, every day, look at this list and appreciate deeply the simple beauty of them all.

---

5   Permission for use of "Comes a Time" lyrics listed in the Permissions and Resources section.

CHAPTER 7

The Cardinal Virtues of Intelligent Investing

"Those who look outside, dream. Those who look inside, awaken."

—*Carl Jung*

"The man who sees me in everything
and everything within me
will not be lost to me, nor
will I ever be lost to him.
He who is rooted in oneness
realizes that I am
in every being; wherever
he goes, he remains in me.
When he sees all beings as equal
in suffering or in joy
because they are like himself,
that man has grown perfect in yoga."

—*Anonymous*, Bhagavad Gita

At this point, we must turn briefly to the nuts and bolts and basic mechanics that lie at the core of both portfolio management and the investment process itself. There are only a limited number of forms that such an explanation can take.

Here is where our groundwork of the spirit can help not only our spiritual growth, but also our financial growth. By achieving an appreciation of the peace within, we can turn our attention to planning appropriate investment decisions. And we can avoid the pitfalls of hasty, emotional moves.

If I were to try and explain the mathematical processes by which two numbers could be added together to reach the total sum of four, my options for discussing that would be limited by the very definition of the subject matter. So it is with basic addition, as well as with portfolio management. Given that, we'll be relying heavily on the work of Harry Markowitz[6], who won a Nobel Prize for his work on the subject.

Any destination can be arrived at via a number of different roads, so throughout this explanation of the core principles of investing, which I have called the Cardinal Virtues of Intelligent Investing, I'll also include my own notes and observation. To begin, we'll examine the Cardinal Virtues themselves.

CARDINAL VIRTUE #1:

Rising Above the Noise/Quitting the Emotional Investment Mind

Despite what some investment professionals would lead you to believe, investing isn't really all that complicated. Part of the illusion of complexity stems from the fact that most people lack an understanding of and familiarity with investment concepts, but it's also true that investment professionals themselves sometimes add to the confusion, believing that they have a vested interest in using intimidating jargon to intentionally muddy the waters. We're going to cut through all of that and explore three different methods that investors use to make decisions about their money, and we'll talk about where you should be with your own approach to your portfolio.

Exhibit 7-1 broadly classifies people according to how

---

6   © Harry Markowitz. Used with the permission of Harry Markowitz.

they make investing decisions, and as you might guess, the first of these, the Noise Method, is commonly used, but wildly ineffective. This is essentially reflexive investing. There's no overarching strategy involved and no tactical thought. It simply describes investors who get caught up in the noise of the day and who allow their emotions to dictate their actions. They chase after hot stocks and market sectors and ignore investments that are undervalued and poised to rise. As a result of their profound lack of focus, they often earn poor returns that fail to get them to their most important financial goals.

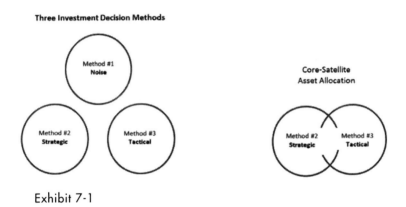

Exhibit 7-1

The sad truth is that most of the investing public uses the Noise Method of investing. It's actually somewhat hard not to, because there's so much noise in the media. Let's face it, for the media, it's all about getting you to come back, and part of what keeps drawing you back is sensationalism. That is what sells newspapers and magazine subscriptions, and at the end of the day, selling is more important to a media outlet than providing good, noise-free information.

A more interesting question is: Why do so many investors consistently make poor, noise-based decisions?

The simple answer is that noise drives emotion. To help you understand the emotions of investing, let's look for a moment at what happens when you hear about a stock.

If you're like most investors, you don't buy the stock right away. You've probably had the experience of losing money on an investment—and did not enjoy the experience—so you're not going to race out and buy that stock the moment you hear it's the latest "sure thing." You're cautious, so you decide to follow it for a while to see how it does. Sure enough, it starts trending upward (see Exhibit 7-2, below).

THE EMOTIONAL CURVE OF INVESTING

Exhibit 7-2

You follow it for a while as it rises. What's your emotion? Confidence. You hope that this might be the one investment that helps you make a lot of money. Let's say it continues its upward trend. You start feeling a new emotion as you begin to consider that this just might be the one. What is the new emotion? It's greed. You decide to buy the stock that day.

You know what happens next. Soon after you buy it, the stock starts to go down, and you feel a new combination of emotions—fear and regret. You're afraid you made a terrible mistake. You promise yourself that if the stock just goes back up to where you bought it, you will never do it again. You don't want to have to tell your spouse or partner about it. You don't care about making money anymore.

Let's say the stock continues to go down. You find yourself with a new emotion. What is it? It's panic. You sell the stock. And what happens next? The stock races to an all-time high.

We're all poorly wired for investing. Emotions are powerful forces that cause you to do exactly the opposite of what you should do. Your emotions lead you to buy high and sell low. If you do that over a long period of time, you'll cause serious damage not just to your portfolio, but, more important, to your financial goals.

DON'T TRY TO TIME THE MARKET

I believe that one of the most difficult ways to increase potential returns is to time the stock market. The classic market timer moves his portfolio in and out of the stock market, hoping to be in during the rising market days and out of the market when prices are falling.

The problem is that no one can reliably predict the future, so it should come as no great surprise that the evidence overwhelmingly demonstrates that such attempts are a losing proposition.

John Bogle, founder of the Vanguard Group of mutual funds, wrote of market timing: "After nearly 50 years in this business, I do not know of anybody who has done it successfully and consistently. I don't even know of anybody who knows anybody who has done it successfully and consistently."

Another reason it is so hard to "time" the markets is that they tend to have bursts of large gains or losses that are concentrated over a relatively short span of time. Exhibit 7-3 on page 82 illustrates that if an investor misses just a few of the best performing trading days, he loses a large percentage of the market's total returns. We believe it is impossible to predict with any degree of reliability when those best (or worst) trading days will occur. Therefore, timing the market can be very difficult.

Good decisions simply are not made during high levels of emotion and stress. Usually we tend to want to get out of the market at times when emotions are high. We need a quiet mind, much like in the wisdom teachings we have been referring to throughout this book. It's important to realize that although we're talking about investing here, lessons learned in other areas of our lives can and do have an influence on our long-term investment results. It is very difficult and risky to time the market. Many people panic when they see reports of a falling stock market. However, staying invested in the market over the long term has historically paid off.

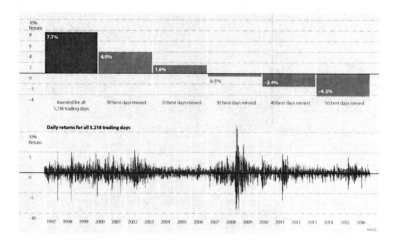

Exhibit 7-3

Although short-term fluctuations seem random, the stock market tends to reflect the overall growth and productivity of the economy in the long term.

Sticking to a carefully planned investment strategy is no different from having a disciplined spiritual practice. Jesus fasted in the desert for 40 days to understand His spiritual path and God's will. Buddha sat under the Bodhi Tree for a similar period before achieving enlightenment and understanding the true nature of reality. Similarly, we need not just react to our emotional minds. Instead, we should allow our minds to settle before making major changes to our investment strategies.

The same media outlets and noise I am suggesting to avoid to help raise our potential investment success can also be avoided and seen for what they are as they relate to our overall peace of mind, perception of reality, and development of spiritual practices. Even outside our investments, there is freedom in not getting caught up in the social media and the cable television's 24/7 onslaught of telling us how to think and what to think about. This will free us from this mind control and allow room in our consciousness for higher mindful inspiration. This can help you to finally hear your own inner voice and gain greater spiritual awareness in the same way that a quiet mind helps your long-term investment success.

Of fundamental importance is the understanding that two of our greatest assets, the intellectual mind and our own instincts, are not always our friends. They can, in some cases, even betray us. This is illustrated in a study conducted annually by Dalbar, a leading financial services market research firm. Dalbar investigates how mutual fund investors' behavior affects the returns they actually earn.

How does the average investor do without professional investment advice? While stocks have historically outperformed other investment classes over the most recent 20-year period, you can see in Exhibit 7-4 the average equity mutual fund investor—someone who has been investing in stocks over that same time period—has not done as well as the market. A big reason for this is thinking too much or rethinking too much when the markets are at extremes. We know that the market has emotional swings over time, moving up and down in an edgy sort of neurotic fashion. Many investors allow their emotional minds to make decisions when stocks are down and sell as well as when stocks are high by buying, which is a recipe for investing disaster. If we can take some of the spiritual lessons from the great wisdom traditions we talked about that are appropriate for finding peace and joy in everyday life, and we apply them to the idea of sticking to a carefully planned-out investment strategy, we can help mitigate the outcome of making poor investment decisions at market extremes.

THE INVESTOR EXPERIENCE

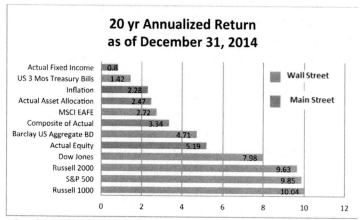

20 yr Annualized Return as of December 31, 2014

	Return	
Actual Fixed Income	0.8	
US 3 Mos Treasury Bills	1.42	
Inflation	2.28	
Actual Asset Allocation	2.47	Wall Street
MSCI EAFE	2.72	Main Street
Composite of Actual	3.34	
Barclay US Aggregate BD	4.71	
Actual Equity	5.19	
Dow Jones	7.98	
Russell 2000	9.63	
S&P 500	9.85	
Russell 1000	10.04	

Source: Dalbar's 21st Annual Quantitation Analysis of Investor Behavior. Used with permission

Exhibit 7-4

STRATEGIC AND TACTICAL METHODS OF INVESTING

Once you have trained your brain to start filtering out the noise, and once you've conditioned yourself to refrain from making important financial decisions on the basis of emotion, the good news is that a couple of other investment approaches begin to reveal themselves. With these, you can begin to build an investment plan that may help you achieve consistent investment success.

Many institutional money management firms use these methods with their clients, which include large corporations and endowments. These methods require orders of magnitude more disciplined than most individual investors are accustomed to, but if you can employ an institutional mindset when it comes to your investments, you have the potential to rise above the noise and possibly enjoy a greater level of investment success than investors who are driven by their emotions.

Broadly speaking, and as outlined in the first graphic we looked at, there are two institutional-class approaches to investment. The first is the Strategic Method of making investment decisions. Strategic investors use a process based on an approach for building portfolios that may provide greater returns for a given level of investment risk. Strategic investors may rebalance those portfolios quarterly to ensure that they maintain the desired combination of return and risk. For the strategic investor, it's all about the broad arc of history, resting their hats on this verdict of history and company fundamentals. If a company's fundamentals are rock solid and they've got a good management team and a proven record of performance, they may be a "fit" in the portfolio. Note here that day-to-day headlines or short-term under—or overvaluations don't even factor into the thinking of the strategic investor. The strategic investor is thinking long-term right from the start.

The second institutional-class approach is the Tactical Method. Tactical investors manage their portfolios differently. Instead of quarterly rebalancing, they look to add value by emphasizing certain asset classes or market sectors that their research efforts tell them are undervalued and offer the potential for above-average returns. Tactical investors then de-emphasize those asset classes or sectors once they become fairly valued by the marketplace. Tactical investors are therefore more opportunistic than strategic investors.

Many in the academic community as well as many institutional investors follow a mix of strategic and tactical methods. Investors who use strategic and tactical methods first research what works, and then follow a rational course of action based on the empirical evidence they've gathered. This allows them to ignore the noise created by the media.

Working with a professional who passionately embodies the concept of helping investors make informed decisions about your money is critical to developing a trusted advisor relationship to promote your success as an investor. Think about that for a moment, and let the full weight and meaning of the sentence above sink in. If the person you're working with is passionate about investing and embodies the concept of helping you, the individual investor, make good, informed decisions about money, then by definition, that's a person who is going to be able to look at your own life's journey and where you ultimately want to go, and then help you chart a course to help make that happen. In order to achieve that, the advisor and the client must be in sync and "on the same wavelength."

To develop this relationship, an advisor must begin with a good understanding of the story of the journey of the investor he's helping and where that story needs to go next and in the longer term, and then he should take steps to help the investor move from away the noise and toward making informed decisions about money, using these prudent investment strategies:

- Strategic investing
- Tactical investing
- Core-satellite asset allocation, which is more or less a hybrid of the strategic and tactical allocations mentioned above

These strategies will help enable you to achieve what is most important to you. Remember, there are no coincidences.

CARDINAL VIRTUE # 2:

Leverage Diversification to Reduce Risk

"Don't put all your eggs in one basket."

Everybody has heard that phrase, and for most people it represents their understanding of diversification. Admittedly, it's a fairly good beginning in terms of understanding diversification, but by itself it does not go far enough and may lead you into an insidious trap if you're not careful.

Our goals are to help protect our clients' wealth, help them protect their purchasing power in the future, and do our best to take steps in discussing with our clients the importance of having enough liquidity available to meet any short—and intermediate-term needs.

It is not enough to simply buy a variety of stocks and call yourself diversified. Part of diversification and part of why it's effective is that, done correctly, it means you're purchasing investments across a variety of industries. If you buy three different technology stocks, for instance, you're not really diversified because tech stocks all tend to be influenced by the same basic factors and will tend to rise and fall together. It is only by diversifying across industry groups that you gain the full benefits of this fundamental aspect of investment.

True diversification also means investing across a number of different asset classes. This can potentially help lower your risk without necessarily sacrificing return. It's impossible to know with certainty which asset classes will perform best in the years ahead, and diversified investors take a balanced approach and stick with it despite volatility in the markets.

My own life's story has revealed to me the dangers inherent in the "all your eggs in one basket" approach to life and living. Those lessons transfer almost perfectly to the sphere of investing. At one point in my life, my business career was more important than my spiritual life. I suffered from what I call insatiable desire. I was never satisfied with my business performance. My ego would raise the bar as soon as I accomplished anything. Remember what Buddha called the root of suffering? That's correct—it's excessive desire. Desire causes suffering. When we are never satisfied, we suffer. Today, I enjoy a much more balanced view of what defines real success. What good is anything without inner peace?

	Before recession Jan 1980–Nov 2007	During recession Dec 2007–Jun 2009	Entire period Jan 1980–Dec 2016
Small stocks	0.72	0.95	0.77
International stocks	0.57	0.93	0.67
Commodities	0.08	0.51	0.21
REITs	0.47	0.83	0.56
Gold	0.05	–0.06	0.04
Long-term corp bonds	0.23	0.34	0.19
Long-term govt bonds	0.18	0.03	0.05
Intermediate-term govt bonds	0.12	–0.32	0.04
Treasury bills	0.00	–0.11	0.02

•Low •Medium •High

Exhibit 7-5(a)

	2002	2003	2004	2005	2006	2007	2008	2009	2010	2011	2012	2013	2014	2015	2016
Highest returns	24.8	56.3	26.0	34.5	32.6	39.8	25.9	79.0	19.2	27.1	18.6	32.4	24.7	1.8	12.0
	17.8	39.2	20.7	14.0	26.9	11.6	10.3	32.5	15.1	9.2	18.0	23.3	13.7	1.4	11.6
	14.2	28.8	14.6	11.9	15.8	10.3	-9.7	26.5	11.8	6.9	17.9	-2.3	6.2	-0.4	9.6
	-6.0	20.7	11.8	7.8	10.5	9.9	-37.0	25.9	10.1	2.1	16.0	-4.5	2.0	-0.7	3.5
	-15.7	19.7	10.9	4.9	6.6	6.5	-43.1	4.2	8.2	-11.7	3.5	-8.3	-1.8	-5.0	1.8
Lowest returns	-22.1	1.4	6.5	-7.3	1.2	5.5	-53.2	-14.9	5.8	-18.2	3.4	-12.8	-4.5	-14.6	1.5

•U.S. stocks •U.S. bonds •International stocks •International bonds •Emerging-market stocks •Emerging-market bonds

Exhibit 7-5(b)

Again, Jesus said it differently: "For what will a man profit if he shall gain the whole world, and lose his soul?"

See Exhibits 7-5(a) and 7-5(b) on pages 87 and 88 which show the historical cycles of asset class performance. Asset allocation and diversification may help investors take advantage of asset classes that are doing well and help diminish the effects of those that are performing poorly.

BE CONSCIOUS OF MAKING THE ASSET ALLOCATION DECISION

Asset allocation is the key component of any prudent investment strategy that attempts to balance risk versus reward by adjusting the percentage of each asset in an investment portfolio according to the investor's risk tolerance, goals, and investment time frame.

It is absolutely essential to have a clear understanding of the different historical risks and returns for different asset classes and to understand the relationship between risk and reward, as these are some of the most important fundamentals of investing. Without an in-depth understanding of these at a minimum, investors never make it across the creek during bear markets without getting thrown from the proverbial horse. This is proven out by the earlier noted Dalbar study. It is not enough to just look at the Ibbotson charts and put together asset class components. A careful assessment of risk is also necessary.

Exhibit 7-6 illustrates that, historically, an effective asset allocation strategy is one of the most important factors impacting the variability (volatility) of investment returns. We simply cannot know for sure what asset class will outperform one year to the next, much like not being able to predict the weather. A simple example I like to use to explain the need to diversify asset classes and individual securities is the island economy: a suntan lotion business would be a good business to own on a sunny tropical island; however, we can diversify our position by also owning an umbrella company to benefit from the inevitable rainy days. We know that the weather changes all the time on tropical islands. One humble fact to be aware of is, once you add a new asset to a portfolio, one may underperform the other. We need to remember the reasons for diversification.

OF OVERWHELMING IMPORTANCE

Importance of Asset Allocation

Asset allocation strategy is one of the most important factors affecting the variability of investment returns.

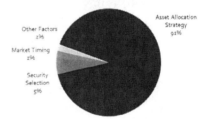

SOURCES OF PORTFOLIO PERFORMANCE[1]

Asset Allocation Strategy 91%

Other Factors 1%

Market Timing 2%

Security Selection 5%

[1]. Roger G. Ibbotson. "Does Asset Allocation Policy Explain 10, 90 or 100 Percent of Performance?" Financial Analyst Journal, January/February 2000; Brinson, Singer and Beebower, "Determination of Performance II: An Update," Financial Analyst Journal, May/June 1991. Based on US pension-fund data from 1977 to 1987

Note: Studies that employ different statistical interpretations produce different results. Real results may vary. Asset allocation does not assure a profit or protect against loss

Exhibit 7-6

It is extremely important to understand how different asset classes behave over time and throughout an investment or economic cycle. Let's take a look at the asset classes that make up an asset allocation plan. An asset class is a group of economic resources sharing similar characteristics, such as riskiness and return. There are many types of assets that may or may not be included in an asset allocation strategy.

Broadly speaking, the two main components of a portfolio are stocks and bonds.

1. *Stock.* The stock (also capital stock) of a corporation constitutes the equity stake of its owners. It is ownership of the company. It represents the residual assets of the company that would be due to stockholders after discharge of all senior claims, such as secured and unsecured debt. Stockholders' equity cannot be withdrawn from the company in a way that is intended to be detrimental to the company's creditors.

2. *Bonds (Fixed Income Instruments).* In finance, a bond is an instrument of indebtedness of the bond issuer to the holders. It is a debt security under which the issuer owes the holders a debt and, depending on the terms of the bond, is obliged to pay them interest (the coupon) and/ or to repay the principal at a later date, termed the maturity date. Interest is usually payable at fixed intervals (semiannual, annual, sometimes monthly).

Thus, a bond is a form of loan or an IOU (sounded out as "I owe you"): The holder of the bond is the lender (creditor), the issuer of the bond is the borrower (debtor), and the coupon is the interest. Bonds carry a lower risk and offer a lower expected return than common stocks. This is especially true of high-quality, short-term bonds.

Bonds and stocks are both securities, but the major difference between the two is that (capital) stockholders have an equity stake in the company (i.e., they are investors), whereas bondholders have a creditor stake in the company (i.e., they are lenders). As creditors, bondholders have absolute priority and will be repaid before stockholders (who are owners) in the event of bankruptcy. Another difference is that bonds usually have a defined term, or maturity, after which the bond is redeemed, whereas stocks are typically outstanding indefinitely.

THE ASSET ALLOCATION DECISION: FOCUS ON ASSET CLASSES

The primary driver of an investment's return is risk. In particular, it is the riskiness of and relationship between the asset classes that make up your portfolio and how you allocate your portfolio among those asset classes. This is what we call the asset allocation decision.

An asset class is a group of similar investments that share impartially defined and common risk/return characteristics. Cash, stocks, and bonds are the most general asset classes. Within these broadly drawn categories are more specific asset classes that narrowly define and capture certain risk factors.

Germane to any asset allocation plan is a focus on broad investment categories rather than individual stocks or bonds. True allocators cite a landmark study involving pension funds.[7]

In 1986, Gary Brinson, L. Randolph Hood, and Gilbert Beebower analyzed the returns of 91 large U.S. pension plans between 1974 and 1983. They concluded that asset allocation explained 90% of the variance in returns. That conclusion was confirmed by the same authors in 1991 after they analyzed a larger database of returns.

Roger Ibbotson and Paul Kaplan published a landmark study[8] in 2001 entitled "Does Asset Allocation Policy Explain 40%, 90%, or 100% of Performance?" The report confirmed that more than 90% of the variation in portfolio return is explained by asset allocation decisions. It is not the selection of individual

---

7 ("Determinants of Portfolio Performance" Brinson, Hood and Beebower, Financial Analysts Journal, July, August 1986)

8 Association for Investment Management and Research; https://corporate. morningstar.com/ib/documents/MethodologyDocuments/IBBAssociates/ AssetAllocationExplain.pdf

stocks or bonds driving performance. Instead, it is the asset allocation that makes the difference in the long term.

The first step toward making an allocation decision is to come to some understanding of your desired mix of cash, stocks, and bonds. Again, this is the single most important investment decision you will make! Some of these asset classes include:

FIXED INCOME ASSET CLASSES

Fixed Income Sectors can be defined as Interest Sensitive, Credit Sensitive, or Municipal:

Treasure Securities	Corporate Bonds	General Obligation
U.S. Agency & GSE	High Yield Bonds	Revenue Bonds
Mortgage-Backed	Foreign Currency Bonds	Pre-refunded Bonds
Zero Coupon Bonds	Emerging Markets Debts	High Yield Bonds
Certificates of Deposit	Preferred Securities	Nontraditional Munis
Short-Term Debt	Convertible Bonds	Taxable Municipal

EQUITY ASSET CLASSES

U.S. Large Stocks

U.S. Large Value Stocks

U.S. Small Stocks

U.S. Small Value Stocks

International Large Stocks

International Large Value Stocks

International Small Stocks

International Small Value Stocks

Emerging Markets Stocks (Large, Small, and Value)

Real Estate Stocks (Domestic and International)

Small-Cap Stocks: market capitalization of less than $1 billion

Mid-Cap Stocks: market capitalization between $1 billion and $5 billion

Large-Cap Stocks: market capitalization greater than $5 billion

CASH

The percentage of your assets invested in cash equivalents (highly liquid, safe, and accessible short-term investments such as T-bills, CDs, and Money Market accounts, all of which offer the lowest risk and least return) should be directly proportional to how quickly you may need to access these funds. Any money you need to put your hands on in less than a year's time should be considered investable in these types of instruments.

BONDS (LOWER RISK/LOWER RETURN) AND STOCKS (HIGHER RISK/HIGHER RETURN)

Because stocks carry more risk than bonds, it follows that they should provide higher returns in the long run. Bonds, therefore, should be seen as tools for smoothing out the volatility of your portfolio. So you might consider restricting your bond holdings to the highest quality, shorter maturity notes, such as short-term U.S. Treasury Bills or high-quality Corporate Bonds. These are typically the safest and least volatile fixed-income asset classes and may serve to help anchor your portfolio.

Bonds have a place in a balanced portfolio, as they serve an important diversifier effect and have been shown to be an important aspect of helping investors meet cash flow needs and weather volatile markets.

TO THINE OWN SELF BE TRUE/KNOWING YOUR INNER SANCTUM

There are two reasons we recommend that you include bonds in your mix:

1. *Your risk tolerance.* Bear markets are very disturbing. They are no joy ride. The markets historically have had many periods when stocks drop by 20%, 30%, 40%, or even more. In recent history, we have experienced some severe bear markets. The three most notable were the 1973/1974, the 2000/2002, as well as the 2008/2009 bear markets. They were very difficult markets to experience without reacting in some fashion. Be sure you can withstand some temporary pain and the inevitable downturns of bear markets. We often tell clients that going through bear markets is part of the price we pay for the long-term returns associated with the stock market. However, we don't want to own more stocks in a portfolio than we are prepared to go through a bear market with. We have to examine cash flow needs as well in the evaluation process. As we have shown, studies conclude that investors tend to panic and sell at or near the bottom of declining markets, which has the effect of "locking in" their losses and causing them to often miss out on the ensuing recovery.

    Investors need to understand and come to grips with their emotional ability to withstand the down years in equities, because there absolutely will be down years. If your portfolio is properly allocated to match your risk tolerance, you'll be better able to maintain your investment discipline and composure and thus enjoy better investment returns over the long term. I like to use the analogy of only getting on a horse from which you won't get thrown midstream: as the Dalbar study points out, most investors never get the results of the market return because they can't make it through a bear market without getting thrown from the horse.

2. *Your life stage.* The phase of life you are in has a lot to do with your asset allocation. The rule of thumb is, "The closer to retirement, the more aware one should be of their overall allocation to stocks." A much better candidate for an asset mix that is more heavily weighted toward riskier (equity) investments is naturally a younger investor. This individual will most likely not need to withdraw money from his/her investment portfolio right away and has more time to weather down-market periods. A younger investor have more future earning capacity as well. He/she should be better able to withstand (emotionally) the short-term ups and downs of the market. One whose earning capacity is limited and who is withdrawing part of his/her portfolio each year for living expenses has to be more cautious, as it relates to the percentage one has allocated to the stock market.

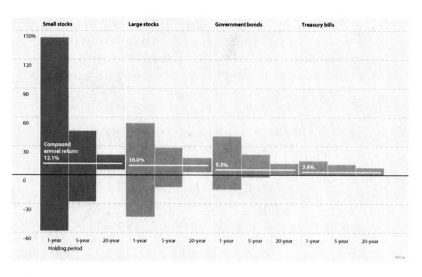

Exhibit 7-7

BAKING THE PIE

> *"Selecting the asset classes for a portfolio constitutes a critically important set of decisions, contributing in large measure to a portfolio's success or failure. Identifying appropriate asset classes requires focus on functional characteristics, considering the potential to deliver returns and to mitigate portfolio risk. Commitment to an equity bias enhances returns, while pursuit of diversification reduces risks. Thoughtful, deliberate focus on asset allocation dominates the agenda of long-term investors."*
>
> —*David Swensen, Chief Investment Officer, Yale University Endowment Fund*

Which specific asset classes should be included in the mix for a U.S. investor? A topic this important should clearly lend itself to a highly detailed conversation with your financial advisor, but a practical place to start is allocating money to domestic large-cap stocks, i.e., stocks included in the S&P 500 index. These 500 companies account for approximately 70% of the market cap of the entire U.S. stock market.

From here, an investor should work with his/her advisor to identify other domestic equity asset classes that would complement and diversify his/her holdings. Depending on the financial goals and risk tolerance, you might recommend including at least some exposure to U.S. small cap and value stocks, as they can potentially increase the expected return and often provide more diversification. Also, real estate investment trusts may serve an investor well in this regard and should be investigated to determine their fit in a portfolio.

CARDINAL VIRTUE #3:

Use Global Diversification to Enhance Returns and Reduce Risk

Investors here in the U.S. tend to favor stocks and bonds of U.S.-based companies. That's because, for many, it's much more comfortable, emotionally, to invest in firms that they know and whose products they use than in companies located on another continent.

Unfortunately, those investors' emotional reactions are causing them to miss out on a way to potentially increase their returns. That's because the U.S. financial market, while the largest in the world, still represents less than half of the total investable capital market worldwide. By looking at overseas investments, you might consider increasing your opportunity to invest in global firms that can help grow your wealth.

Global diversification in your portfolio may also help reduce overall risk. One reason is that American equity markets and international markets generally do not move together. In investing, there is a correlation between risk and return; individual stocks of companies around the world with similar risk have the same expected rate of return. However, they don't get there in the same manner or at the same time. The price movements between international and U.S. asset classes are often dissimilar, so investing in both might increase your portfolio's diversification.

TYING IT ALL TOGETHER

As you can see, there are a number of factors involved in the asset allocation decision-making process, and the sections that follow in this chapter will add yet more wrinkles to the equation. Even so, now is a good time to reflect on your own life's journey and see the obvious parallels between your story and asset allocation decision making. Without question, there have been times in your life when you've found yourself at a crossroads because life has presented you with two or more choices, all potentially good, and each carrying a different level of risk and reward. Perhaps you had to choose between taking a chance by going to work with a small, feisty start-up firm with lower pay and an uncertain future, but nearly endless potential for growth, versus going to work for a family friend at a large, well-established multinational company with better pay and greater job security, but with only limited opportunities for advancement. Which did you choose? Do you find yourself wishing that you had chosen differently? To thine own self be true.

I needed to trust the will of God when I surrendered myself to stop drinking alcohol when I was 21. By surrendering myself, I was given the greatest gifts ever: peace of mind and the grace of God in my life. Little did I know what this one decision would mean for my life and ultimately for my soul. We have to live our truth in all of our decisions.

WHETHER OR NOT TO PARTNER WITH A TRUSTED ADVISOR

An important consideration is whether you are going to manage your money yourself or will work with a skilled and competent financial advisor/wealth manager. Financial planning and wealth management can be complex, and your entire financial future is at stake. If you plan on investing on your own, you need to understand that it can be difficult, time-consuming, and emotionally draining for you. Many individuals do not have the crucial skills and knowledge to manage their own investment assets. You need to ask yourself if you have access to the resources that financial advisors and wealth managers have on a global basis. Creating and maintaining a diversified investment portfolio takes talent in order to avoid asset duplication and to minimize taxes. Plus, the ongoing monitoring of your portfolio is an enormous task that must be performed carefully. You may have certain life transitions that need to be considered as you monitor your portfolio, and, if so, you must rebalance the assets at those times. You need tools to implement the process, and it will be very challenging to do this unless you have the same resources available to professional advisors.

CARDINAL VIRTUE #4:

Seek Lower Volatility to Enhance Returns
The Geometry of Portfolio Returns and Volatility

Volatility represents uncertainty. If you have two investment portfolios with the same average or arithmetic return, the portfolio with less volatility can have a greater compound rate of return. Let's assume you are considering two mutual funds. Each has had an average arithmetic rate of return of 8% over five years. How would you determine which fund is better? Either way, you would probably expect to have the same ending wealth value. But that would be true only if the two funds have the same degree of volatility. If one fund is more volatile than the other, the compound returns and ending values with less volatility can have a higher compound return.

You can see this works in Exhibit 7-8. Two equal investments can have the same arithmetic rate of return, but have different ending values because of volatility. You want to design your portfolio so that it has as little volatility as necessary to help you achieve your financial goals. Exhibit 7-8 shows two portfolios with the same average return. As a prudent investor, you want the less volatile ride of the portfolio on the left side, not only because it helps you ride out the emotional curve, but also more importantly because with it you have the potential to create more wealth toward your goals.

	Consistent Investment		Volatile Investment	
EXHIBIT 3 **LESS VOLATILITY = GREATER WEALTH**				
Year	Rate of Return	Ending Value	Rate of Return	Ending Value
1	8%	$108,000	30%	$130,000
2	8%	$116,640	-20%	$104,000
3	8%	$125,971	25%	$130,000
4	8%	$136,049	-20%	$104,000
5	8%	$146,933	25%	$130,000
Arithmetic return	8%		8%	
Compound return	8%		5.39%	

Source: CEG Worldwide.

Exhibit 7-8

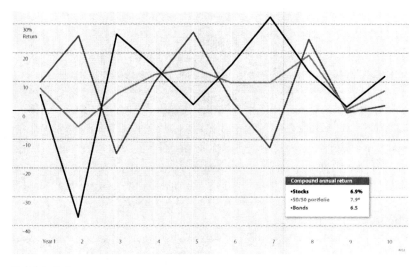

Exhibit 7-9

In Exhibit 7-9, the hypothetical sample asset classes shown on this chart —Asset Class A and Asset Class B—both have volatile returns, which means that their returns vary a great deal from year to year: one year the performance is up, the next year it is down, and so on. The performance of the two hypothetical asset classes is also not correlated. Asset classes that are correlated have investment returns that move in the same direction—either up or down—at the same time. As you can see here, these asset classes are uncorrelated—which means that when the returns are up for one asset class, they are down for the other. Either one of these asset classes would take an individual who invested only in one of the asset classes on quite a ride from year to year with his/her investment returns. However, as you can see in the example on the second chart of Exhibit 7-9, if our hypothetical investor were to split his/her money between these two asset classes in his/her portfolio, the return on the portfolio would be much less volatile from year to year—without the wild swings in performance we saw from the asset classes on their own. In brief, such a split tends to smooth out the volatility of the assets when they are considered individually.

MEASURING RISK—LET'S LOOK AT HOW THE PROS DO IT

As mentioned briefly earlier, the "standard deviation" is the tool used by professionals to measure risk. This is a statistical measure of degree. In particular, it measures the degree to which numbers in a series differ from the average. Under normal conditions, you expect to see roughly two-thirds of numbers falling within a single standard deviation of the mean (the average).

Standard deviation quantifies the volatility associated with a portfolio's returns. The statistic measures the variation in returns around the mean return. Unlike beta, which measures volatility relative to the aggregate market, standard deviation measures the absolute volatility of a portfolio's return.

Measurement of the total volatility, or risk, of your portfolio standard deviation tells how widely your portfolio's returns have varied around the average over a period of time. A smaller standard deviation indicates a lower level of risk.

Some value investors consider risk to be specifically related to price and a security's intrinsic value when evaluating individual businesses. They may look to pay only a percentage of that intrinsic value. For purposes of portfolio analysis, we will focus on the statistical measure of standard deviation.

When considering matters of asset allocation, though, it is insufficient to merely look at the type of investment vehicles one has to choose from. The investor must also evaluate the risk that each type of investment and each individual investment under a given asset class might carry. Below, we'll examine the major ones, which include:

Maturity Risk—Long-term bonds tend to have more risk, and thus price volatility, than shorter-term bonds, all else being equal. This makes a certain logical sense because a loan made for a term of 10 years carries more inherent risk than a loan made for a term of only one month. A lot can happen in 10 years.

Market Risk—This is the risk inherent in any securities market. As such, this risk is non-diversifiable. Professionals call this risk "systemic" as it relates to the overall market. If you own stock and the market itself trends sharply downward, it isn't likely to matter how well your company is performing; its stock price will likely be dragged down with the broader market. In other words, a rising tide lifts all ships, and a lower tide lowers all ships. Though there are always companies that are in an exceptional growth stage that buck the trend, they are few and far between.

Inflation Risk—Most bonds' payments are fixed. But prices of the things you need to buy keep on going up. The longer a bond's term, the greater the chance that the payout won't keep pace with inflation.

Credit risk—This is the risk that your bond issuer will be unable to make its payments on time, or at all. U.S. Treasury bonds are considered to have virtually no credit risk, while high-yield, or "junk," bonds—issued by companies with weak finances—have high credit risk.

Interest rate risk—Though a bond's life span and interest payments are fixed—thus the term "fixed-income" investment—its overall return can vary based on changes in the economy and the markets. Bonds are traded just like stocks, so changes in the economy and the markets can cause bond prices to rise or fall. Bond prices move in the opposite direction of interest rates—that is, when interest rates rise, bond prices fall. The longer the term of the bond, the greater the price fluctuation that results from any change in interest rates. (Note that price fluctuations matter only if you intend to sell a bond before maturity, or if you invest in a bond fund whose manager trades regularly.)

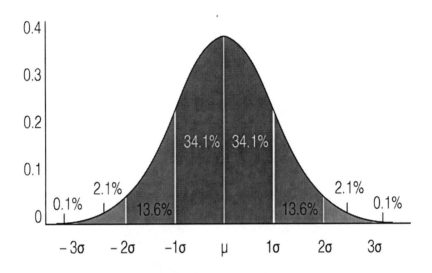

KEY DEFINITIONS

Expected rate of return is typically calculated as the risk-free rate of return plus the risk premium associated with that equity investment.

Standard deviation is a description of how far from the mean (average) the historical perform-ance of an investment has been. It is a measure of an investment's volatility.

Correlation coefficients measure the dissimilar price movements among asset classes by quantify-ing the degree to which they move together in time, degree and direction.

Exhibit 7-10

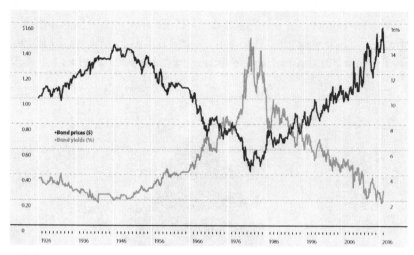

Exhibit 7-11

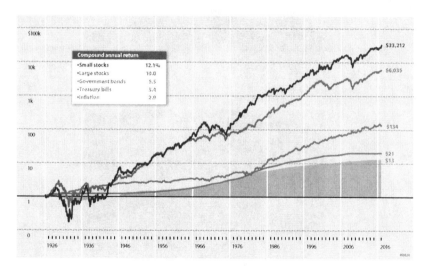

Exhibit 7-12

There are also other types of risk, and the common similarity is uncertainty of future results.

THE RELATIONSHIP BETWEEN RISK AND RETURN

Many investors spend a great deal of time and effort in an attempt to find individual securities that are undervalued. In reality, when great individual opportunities do exist, they are notoriously difficult to take advantage of.

In the 1970s, Roger Ibbotson and Rex Sinquefield did extensive studies of capital market returns. Their revolutionary work clearly illustrates the long-term relationship between risk and reward and provides us with the intellectual framework of supporting one asset class over another.

As a reminder, an "asset class" is a group of similar investment securities with similar, objectively defined risk and return characteristics. See Exhibit 7-12. It extends Ibbotson and Sinquefield's original research through the end of 2016 and shows the relative returns and growth since 1926 of a single dollar invested in major asset classes and inflation.

SIZE AND STYLE: THE FOOD GROUPS OF ASSET CLASSES

Small Companies vs. Large

Notice the higher returns in the Exhibit 7-12 of small cap stocks. There is a body of research that shows that, over a long investment horizon, small cap stocks have outperformed their large cap brethren. This underscores perfectly how risk and return are related. Small companies tend to be riskier than large ones, and this is borne out by the behavior of their stocks, as small cap stocks are riskier than large cap stocks.

The fact that small company stocks have outperformed large company stocks is a reflection of risk known as "The Size Effect." The reward for taking greater risks in the efficiently functioning capital markets is a higher rate of return.

Likewise, stocks (offered by companies large and small) are relatively riskier than bonds, and therefore it is no wonder that large and small company stocks have returned more than bonds.

Although bonds or T-bills could outperform stocks in any particular year, most long-term investors know better than to look at single-year results. The verdict of historical data and investment theory strongly suggests that a risk and return trade-off will prevail, and this paradigm should carry the day over time.

	2007	2008	2009	2010	2011	2012	2013	2014	2015	2016
Highest returns	19.7 MG	-31.7 SV	44.4 LG	31.3 SG	2.2 LV	18.3 SV	42.2 MV	14.4 LG	7.7 LG	28.0 SV
	12.3 LG	-35.9 MV	42.0 MG	27.7 MG	1.6 LG	13.0 LG	41.9 SG	11.5 MV	-0.2 SG	25.2 MV
	11.1 SG	-36.1 LV	40.3 SV	26.0 SV	-0.7 DP	17.6 MV	35.9 DP	10.0 SV	-0.7 MG	18.9 LV
	4.8 DP	-38.6 DP	36.0 MV	22.2 DP	-1.0 SG	16.2 DP	35.7 SV	9.8 MG	-1.0 DP	15.0 DP
	-0.4 LV	-39.9 SG	34.5 DP	20.6 MV	-1.8 SV	15.8 MG	34.1 MG	9.6 DP	-1.4 LV	9.6 SG
	-5.5 MV	-41.9 LG	33.0 SG	14.7 LV	-2.3 MG	14.5 SG	32.5 LG	9.2 LV	-2.6 MV	6.5 MG
Lowest returns	-8.1 SV	-46.3 MG	11.4 LV	12.9 LG	-2.6 MV	12.9 LV	28.9 LV	2.5 SG	-8.6 SV	1.0 LG

•Large growth (LG) •Large value (LV) •Mid growth (MG) •Mid value (MV) •Small growth (SG) •Small value (SV) •Diversified portfolio (DP)

Exhibit 7-13

INVESTOR DECISION: GROWTH OR VALUE?

One of the nice features of the stock market is that there is a huge range of choices investors have when making an investment decision. Unfortunately, this flexibility also results in tough decisions, especially when it comes to fundamental investment strategies, such as the choice between growth and value. To help make that decision a little easier, let's look at each investment type in more detail.

VALUE STOCKS

The idea of value investing has its roots in the work of Benjamin Graham. The strategy behind this concept is an approach to selecting stocks that appear to be underpriced by the market. This may include companies that have low price-to-earnings ratios, or high dividend yields. Because value stocks are selling at relatively low ratios, investors feel these companies are being ignored by the market. Investors believe such stocks are "bargains," because they are priced below what fundamental analysis would indicate is a "fair" amount.

This important characteristic in equity markets is referred to as "The Value Effect." These are undervalued companies and may have some kind of negative headline affecting them, such as a product recall or a product scare, or they are in a maturing industry with slower perceived earnings growth.

GROWTH STOCKS

Generally, a growth stock is one that is expected to generate earnings at a rate that exceeds their industry's average, as well as the average of the overall economy. These companies usually possess a competitive advantage that allows them to generate these above-average profits. This advantage might include a patent, manufacturing scale, or loyal customers.

Growth stocks will usually not pay dividends; instead, they will quickly reinvest profits into new capital projects that will further increase profits. Investors in these companies pay little attention to the stock's price, choosing instead to concentrate on future earnings potential.

Growth stocks may be in a highly popular industry or may be growing currently at a very healthy pace. Growth stocks tend to have high prices relative to their earnings and high price-to-book values. Very often, their valuations will return to the average as a fad or new technology is eclipsed, or is exploited by others.

Long-term investors who can withstand the greater volatility inherent to riskier asset classes have an opportunity to be compensated over time with higher returns, if history is any indication. But please note and keep in mind that risk and return are related!

DESIGN EFFICIENT PORTFOLIOS—THE HOLY GRAIL OF PORTFOLIO MANAGEMENT

How do you decide which investments to use and in what combinations? Since 1972, major institutions have been using a money management concept known as Modern Portfolio Theory. It was developed at the University of Chicago by Harry

Markowitz and Merton Miller, and later expanded by Stanford professor William Sharpe. Markowitz, Miller, and Sharpe subsequently won the Nobel Prize in Economic Sciences for their contribution to investment methodology.

EFFICIENT PORTFOLIOS

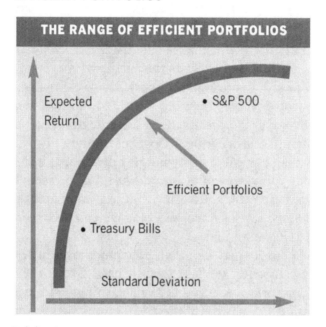

Exhibit 7-14

The process of developing a strategic portfolio using Modern Portfolio Theory is mathematical in nature and can appear daunting. It's important to remember that math is nothing more than an expression of logic, so as you examine the process, you can readily see the commonsense approach that it takes—which is counterintuitive to conventional and over-commercialized investment thinking. Markowitz stated that for every level of risk, there is some optimum combination of investments that will give the highest rate of return. The combinations of investments exhibiting this optimal risk/reward trade-off form the "efficient frontier" line. The efficient frontier is determined by calculating the expected rate of return, standard deviation, and correlation coefficient for each asset class and using this information to identify the portfolio with the highest expected return at each incremental level of risk. See Exhibit 7-14.

By plotting each investment combination, or portfolio, representing a given level of risk and expected return, we are able to describe mathematically a series of points, or "efficient portfolios." This line forms the efficient frontier. Most investor portfolios fall significantly below the efficient frontier. Portfolios such as the S&P 500, which is often used as a proxy for the market, fall below the line when several asset classes are compared. Investors may be able to get the same rates of return with an asset class portfolio with much less risk, or higher rates of return for the same level of risk. Assets that move independently are uncorrelated, and those that move in opposite directions are called negatively correlated.

Please note the chart from Exhibit 7-9. The exhibit illustrates the benefit of blending two hypothetical asset classes that are negatively correlated. Asset A has different risk and return characteristics than Asset B, and therefore their prices move in opposite directions (when A declines, then B rises, and vice versa).

The line labeled Combined Asset Classes that runs down the center illustrates a blended portfolio that holds both of these assets equally. The blended portfolio has lower volatility (i.e., lower standard deviation) than either individual asset alone.

This is an important component of Modern Portfolio Theory. The concept was introduced in 1952 by the Nobel Laureate economist Harry Markowitz.[9] Markowitz first described this idea using individual stocks, but the concept works equally well with mutual funds or entire asset classes.

This concept underscores another very important tenet of investing: focus on the performance of your portfolio as a whole, rather than the returns of its individual components. Do not be discouraged when in any given period some asset classes do not do as well as others.

---

9   Markowitz, H., 1952, Portfolio Selection, Journal of Finance 7, 77-91

USE ASSET CLASSES

Today, with the use of highly advanced state-of-the-art computer models and programs, a financial advisor can evaluate the historical risk/return trend of dissimilar asset classes and use this information to construct a portfolio that maximizes expected returns for any given level of risk. Exhibit 7-15 illustrates this concept. Higher risk/return portfolios generally have a higher percentage allocation in stocks. You can see that the risk level diminshes as the initial stock market exposure (up to about 20%) is added to the 100% bond portfolio. So, shown here are the benefits of diversification available from adding riskier assets that do not move in perfect unison with other assets in your portfolio. By having a strong risk tolerance discussion with you, a good advisor will help you know yourself before engaging.

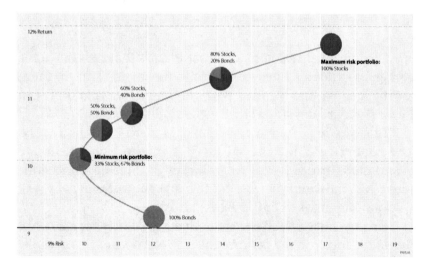

Exhibit 7-15

CARDINAL VIRTUE #5:

Stay Disciplined in Different and Difficult Markets

In the stock market, extended periods of upward price movements are called secular bull markets. Lengthy periods of downward movements are called secular bear markets. Regardless of whether the market is in a secular bull or a secular bear period, investors still need to work toward achieving their financial goals.

The key to navigating the ever-changing market environment is to stay focused on your goals, long-term and short-term. Typically, investors tend to think and act differently in bear markets than they do in bull markets when they feel much more aggressive toward their investments. Rational and disciplined investors understand that to be successful, they need to stay focused on their goals, both their long-term goals and their near-term goals.

A disciplined approach to asset allocation is another key to investment success. That's because certain market segments and asset classes tend to stay healthy even when the broader market is ill. Having the freedom to emphasize those areas of the market that offer some of the best prospects will help keep your investment plan on track during bull and bear markets.

Benjamin Graham, the great Wall Street legend and author of *The Intelligent Investor*, once commented, "The stock market is an expensive place to find out who you are." Again, it cannot be emphasized enough how important it is to know yourself and your risk tolerance ahead of time, before engaging in the markets. The Dalbar study and many others similar to it have shown that most investors never get across the creek in bear markets without getting thrown from the horse midstream. Therefore, it is wise to consider holding only that amount of your portfolio in the stock market that you can stand to carry through the inevitable bear markets that are part of life on Wall Street.

It amounts to having grace and a cool head under pressure. Sometimes when the going gets tough, we panic and give up when we should stay the course. If you want to succeed in investing, you must practice this. We have to run the psychological lifeboat drills before the bear market comes. I cannot overstate enough the impact of investor behavior on long-term performance. It is much more important to get the allocation right than to be on the fastest horse if you're only going to get thrown from it later.

CARDINAL VIRTUE #6:

Rebalance to Original Allocation

This may be more difficult than it sounds, but as our portfolios get out of balance from their original targeted asset allocation, we need to be disciplined to rebalance back to original allocation. Again, our emotional mind may resist and want to let winners run, such as what happens during a strong bull market in stocks. However, we have to be clinical and use this important risk protection strategy. A simple strategy of rebalancing back to the original target once a year can go a long way in protecting a portfolio from drifting into a higher risk allocation.

This also encourages investors, in a natural and orderly way, to sell high and buy low. The more clinical the discipline, the better.

THE ART OF REBALANCING

Periodic Rebalancing: Rebalance back to original target allocation on a fixed schedule—annually, quarterly, monthly.

Threshold Rebalancing: Rebalance when the allocation deviates beyond a certain tolerance range (i.e., plus or minus 5%) and bring back to original target allocation.

Range Rebalancing: Rebalance when the allocation deviates beyond a certain tolerance range and bring the allocation back within the range instead of the original target.

Active Rebalancing: Rebalance as needed, based on analysis of market conditions—similar to tactical asset allocation, which also to exploit shorter-term changes in market values.

Rebalancing tends to reinforce one of the main benefits of diversification: the tendency of returns on different asset classes to offset each other over time. By staying close to their target mix, investors may have the opportunity to reduce portfolio volatility.

> *"Truth undermines the self to which we so desperately cling. The truth is not hidden from us, we are hiding from it."*
>
> —*Kabbalah proverb*

CONTEMPLATION

Close your eyes, and take a few soft, gentle deep breaths. Drop into the empty cup of your heart, and breathe in the Living Truth, the Holy Presence. Be bigger than the world and older than market cycles and seasons. Allow yourself to experience a feeling of Eternal Wealth, a wealth that encompasses the feeling of eternity. Practice this every day—morning immediately upon awakening and night before sleep. The very last thoughts and the very first thoughts we think on any given day absolutely define our lives. Fortify this by rereading daily your list of things that bring you genuine happiness.

DISCLAIMERS

The views expressed herein are those of the author and do not necessarily reflect the views of his employer or its affiliates. All opinions are subject to change without notice. Neither the information provided nor any opinion expressed constitutes a solicitation for the purchase or sale of any security. Past performance is no guarantee of future results.

This material does not provide individually tailored investment advice. It has been prepared without regard to the individual financial circumstances and objectives of persons who receive it. The strategies and/or investments discussed in this material may not be suitable for all investors. The appropriateness of a particular investment or strategy will depend on an investor's individual circumstances and objectives.

Interest accrued on municipal bonds is generally exempt from federal income tax. However, some bonds may be subject to the alternative minimum tax (AMT). Typically, state tax exemption applies if securities are issued within one's state of residence, and local tax exemption typically applies if securities are issued within one's city of residence.

Bonds are affected by a number of risks, including fluctuations in interest rates, credit risk, and prepayment risk. In general, as prevailing interest rates rise, fixed income securities prices will fall. Bonds face credit risk if a decline in an issuer's credit rating, or creditworthiness, causes a bond's price to decline. Finally, bonds can be subject to prepayment risk. When interest rates fall, an issuer may choose to borrow money at a lower interest rate, while paying off its previously issued bonds. As a consequence, underlying bonds will lose the interest payments from the investment and will be forced to reinvest in a market where prevailing interest rates are lower than when the initial investment was made. NOTE: High yield bonds are subject to additional risks, such as increased risk of default and greater volatility, because of the lower credit quality of the issues.

Diversification does not guarantee a profit or protect against a loss.

International investing may not be suitable for every investor and is subject to additional risks, including currency fluctuations, political factors, withholding, lack of liquidity, the absence of adequate financial information, and exchange control restrictions impacting foreign issuers. These risks may be magnified in emerging markets.

REITs are subject to special risk considerations similar to those associated with the direct ownership of real estate. Real estate valuations may be subject to factors such as changing general and local economic, financial, competitive, and environmental conditions. REITs may not be suitable for every investor.

Dividend income from REITs will generally not be treated as qualified dividend income and therefore will not be eligible for reduced rates of taxation. Readers should seek advice based on their particular circumstances from an independent tax advisor.

CHAPTER 8

The Yoga of Wealth Management

"Reality is that which is as it is. It transcends speech and lies beyond such expression as existence and nonexistence."

—*Sri Ramana Maharshi*

"Most men lead lives of quiet desperation and go to the grave with the song still in them."

—*Henry Thoreau*

"You can't solve your problems with the same consciousness that created them."

—*Albert Einstein*

TAKING A CLIENT-DRIVEN HOLISTIC APPROACH

Money means different things to different people. Each of us has different goals. You may want to achieve financial freedom so that you never have to work again—even if you plan on working the rest of your life. You may want to make a top-flight college education possible for your children or grandchildren. You may want to provide the seed capital that will give your children or grandchildren a great start in life, whether that's with a home or a business. You may dream of a vacation home on the beach or in the mountains. Or you may have achieved tremendous success throughout your career and want to leave behind an enduring legacy that will enable your favorite charity to continue its work.

Whatever your goals are, you need a framework for making decisions about your money that will help enable you to achieve what is important to you. Chances are good that you have a wide range of financial goals, as well as diverse financial challenges.

Common sense tells us that such a broad range of issues requires a broad, comprehensive outlook. It's for this reason that most affluent clients want their financial advisors to help them with more than just investments. They want real wealth management—a complete approach to addressing their entire financial lives.

> "When reality explodes in you, you may call it the experience of God, or rather, it is God experiencing you. God knows you when you know yourself. Reality is not the result of a process; it is an explosion. It is definitely beyond the mind, but all you can do is to know your mind well. Not that the mind will help you, but by knowing your mind, you may avoid your mind disabling you. You have to be very alert, or else your mind will play false with you. It is like watching a thief—not that you expect anything from a thief, but you do not want to be robbed. In the same way you need to give a lot of attention to the mind without expecting anything from it."
>
> —Sri Nisargadatta Maharaj

As you've probably noticed, many financial firms these days say that they offer wealth management. The trouble is that some of these firms just provide investment management and offer a couple of extra services—such as college education planning and estate planning—and call that wealth management. The challenge for anyone who wants help addressing his or her comprehensive financial needs is to find a firm that provides true wealth management.

OUR WEALTH MANAGEMENT FORMULA

One of the most important financial responsibilities that I have every day is helping clients to not outlive their money. That's the Wealth Management Consultative Approach.[10]

We use a wealth management formula that looks like this:

$$WM=IC+AP+RM$$

Wealth Management equals Investment Consulting plus Advanced Planning plus Relationship Management.

Here is the interpretation of the formula:

IC = INVESTMENT CONSULTING

Investment consulting (IC) is the management of investments over time to help achieve financial goals.

It requires advisors to deeply understand their clients' most important challenges and then to design an investment plan that takes their clients' time horizons and tolerance for risk into account, and that describes an approach that will help enable clients to possibly achieve what is most important to them. It also requires advisors to monitor both the clients' portfolios and their financial lives over time so that they can make adjustments

---

10   The Informed Investor. © CEG Worldwide, LLC. All rights reserved; Reprinted with the permission of CEG Worldwide, LLC

to the investment plan as needed. It includes:

- Portfolio performance analysis
- Risk evaluation
- Asset allocation
- Assessment of impact of costs
- Assessment of impact of taxes
- Investment plan

The Investment Plan is an important part of the wealth management process. It takes into account the percentage of stock, percentage of bonds, percentage in cash, and percentage in alternatives that should be in the portfolio. It doesn't mean you can't make changes as your life changes, but you need to at least have a plan. As we discussed in the past chapter, many investors don't know their exposure to stocks versus bonds versus cash versus alternatives. They don't know their asset allocation. As good advisors do the plan and evaluate risk tolerance, they also look at the budget. Then they create a plan to follow the asset allocation stated in the planning process. A plan is important to have when you are going through good times, when it is tempting to stray toward the hottest sectors, and in bad times when the short-term downturn may cause you to want to head for the exits.

AP = ADVANCED PLANNING

Advanced Planning also includes this formula:

AP = WE + WT +WP + CG

Advanced planning (AP) goes beyond investments to look at all the other aspects that are important to your financial life. We break it down into four parts: wealth enhancement, wealth transfer, wealth protection, and charitable giving.

The AP (Advanced Planning) formula can be interpreted like this:

WE (Wealth Enhancement: tax mitigation and cash-flow planning) +

WT (Wealth Transfer: transferring wealth effectively; may not be within a family) +

WP (Wealth Protection: risk mitigation, legal structures and transferring risk to insurance company) +

CG (Charitable Giving: maximizing charitable impact)

You have to protect yourself by doing Advanced Planning. For example, if you are a young family, you need to plan for insurance protection.

Wealth Enhancement—The first concern: mitigating or minimizing income and taxes and maximizing cash flow. You should start with a review of recent tax returns to determine a baseline, then perform a current year tax assessment. Your benefits plan should then be evaluated. At this point, your education funding plan for your children or for your grandchildren should be assessed as well. We strive to have tax-efficient, tax-free vehicles such as municipal bonds. Tax-free municipal bonds have been one of the best after-tax fixed income asset classes historically.[11]

Wealth Transfer—First, identify your wealth transfer preferences. Ask yourself these questions: Where do you want the money to go? Are there special circumstances within your family? Do you have any children who might be particularly successful or who may need financial assistance? Do you have a child (or children) who has special needs considerations? It's smart to start by identifying the preferences that you have up front.

Next, it's time to review the existing estate planning documents that you have in place and identify any special situations, such as a

---

family dynamic. You want to confirm that you have correct titling of your assets. If you have estate planning documents in place, you will want to confirm that you funded the trusts that were intended to be funded and made any titling changes that were intended to have been made. You also need to document your wishes regarding end of life issues. Do you want heroic measures to be taken if you're incapacitated? There are many other details around those considerations that need to be discussed.

Wealth Protection—Wealth protection is about protecting ourselves and our loved ones and protecting our confidential information, our financial assets, and our property from being wrongly or improperly taken. This is Advanced Planning Concern #3.

First, brainstorm with your family members and/or with your other professional advisors about the different risks you have, what exposures you have, and then quantify them. Next, it's important to leverage asset protection strategies, which could be legal structures and titling of assets for asset protection. Then you want to always get a second opinion on major financial transactions, just to make sure you are not overlooking any risks.

After that, you need to confirm that your life insurance is adequate, evaluate your property-casualty insurance, and consider umbrella liability coverage. Also verify that your health and disability coverage is adequate. You will want to consider long-term care insurance and evaluate your commercial insurance coverage.

Charitable Giving—The first step, of course, is to determine your charitable intent. The most basic way to make a charitable difference is through volunteering time and/or making small, direct donations. However, in some cases, more sophisticated strategies should be considered in conjunction with the donations. Perhaps you should think about a bequest. Consider community foundations, private foundations, donor-advised funds, and life insurance in a charitable context. Additional strategies include charitable gift annuities, charitable remainder trusts, or charitable lead trusts. You'll need to educate yourself about these strategies or find a skilled wealth manager, CPA, estate attorney, or other professional.

RM = RELATIONSHIP MANAGEMENT

RM = CRM + PNRM is the formula and can be interpreted as follows:

RM (Relationship Management) =

CRM (Client Relationship Management) +

PNRM (Professional Network Relationship Management)

Relationship management (RM) is the final element of the wealth management process. True wealth managers are focused on building relationships within three groups, the first and most obvious of which is their clients. To address their clients' needs effectively, they must foster solid, trusted relationships with them. The second group wealth managers must manage is a network of financial professionals they can call in to address specific client needs. Third, wealth managers must be able to work effectively with their clients' other professional advisors, such as their attorneys and accountants.

THE WEALTH MANAGEMENT CONSULTATIVE PROCESS[12]

There are five steps in the wealth management consultative process. They are:

First Step: Discovery Meeting

It's important to start with a "discovery meeting" which is something you can do on your own or with the help of a wealth manager. First, develop a total personal/family profile to look at

---

12   The Informed Investor. © CEG Worldwide, LLC. All rights reserved; Reprinted with the permission of CEG Worldwide, LLC

where you are now and where you want to go. That total profile should be divided into seven sections: values, relationships, goals, financial information and assets, advisors, process, and interests.

You need to clearly understand your values. What is important about money to you personally? What are your three biggest financial concerns?

What are the most important relationships you have? They can be your parents, siblings, children, friends, or people in the community who are very important to you. One of your most important relationships may even be an organization or an entity to which you have strong ties, such as a religious organization or church.

Next, you want to think about your goals. Where do you want to be in 10 years, in 15 years? What would you like to achieve going forward?

Then you want to look at your financial situation and take an inventory of your assets and your liabilities.

Now list your professional advisors who have a seat at your table in helping you make smart decisions. Who are your professional advisors?

Research shows that a vast majority of investors lack a process for reaching their goals, and surprisingly, they don't believe that their financial advisor has an organized process to solve all of their challenges. So what's the process you're going to use to make sure you stay on track for achieving your goals?

Something else that is essential to your total profile—what do you want to do when you are not working? What do you enjoy doing, and what are your interests?

After you construct your total profile, you will have a clear understanding of where you are now, where you want to go, and what the gaps are that exist.

Second Step: Wealth Management Plan Meeting

Now you need to develop an investment strategy and solutions to your other wealth management issues. During the wealth management meeting or meetings, overall key concerns from a wealth management perspective are discussed, and the investment plan is drafted.

After the meeting (if you are working with a competent and skilled wealth manager) and once the investment plan is drafted, we advise our own clients to take it home, digest it, and bring it back to the next meeting with any questions. If you're doing your own wealth management planning, ideally put the plan aside for a week, then review it to make sure it accurately reflects where you are now and where you want to go, and that it's aligned with your risk/return profile.

Third Step: Mutual Commitment Meeting

We have a mutual commitment meeting with our clients as part of our five-step process. In this step, we look at the draft of the investment plan, the key concerns of the wealth management issues, and then we do any necessary fine-tuning. There may be issues that are unresolved on both sides, so this is the time for you to ask any questions, and it's when we typically ask questions and express any concerns about moving forward as well. We may decide that we are not a 100% good fit for each other. Then both parties make a decision, and if it is a good fit, the working agreement is formalized.

Now it's time to put the plan into place.

To do this, your expert team of accountants, attorneys, and other professionals should meet to review your total family profile. Their job is to brainstorm about actions that you should take to address the Four Advanced Planning Concerns (wealth enhancement, wealth transfer, wealth protection, and charitable giving) and then prioritize these actions for your review. This is something you should do if you don't have a wealth manager handling it for you.

Fourth Step: Strategy Implementation Meeting

In this meeting, you need to prioritize and set timelines for implementing the priorities in each of the Advanced Planning areas. There is a priority decision-making process for wealth transfer, wealth protection, wealth enhancement, and charitable giving. You need to prioritize these now during the Implementation Meeting.

Fifth Step: Regular Progress Meetings

Once you've completed the process, it's important to schedule regular progress meetings. Schedule them for yourself or schedule them with your wealth manager at a frequency that makes sense for your situation, whether it's monthly, quarterly, or semiannually—but at the absolute minimum, annually. Either way, be sure you're having regular progress meetings. Every time you do this, you should review these three things:

- Has anything changed personally, professionally, or financially?
- Are you on track with your investments?
- Is there any fine-tuning that needs to be done?
- What Advanced Planning strategies and tactics are in process right now? What's the status? Are there any new strategies or tactics that should be implemented now?

Remember, whether you have a large family or you're single, whether you are an entrepreneur who owns a large business or you're simply earning a paycheck, you are responsible for making all of these major decisions.

WHAT DO WE MEAN BY AMAZING GRACE?

When we are in harmony with Divinity—or, as the Hindus call it, Brahman—and are in love with life and in union with God, we are referring to an amazing grace that can change hearts. It can change manifested forms and what becomes of our lives. It transcends all limitations of the physical world, and life becomes gracefully easy and a magical experience of wonder. Having a grateful heart creates the energy that in turn helps us create the grace in our lives. Grace, gratitude, and appreciation for what we have are like magnetism, and we are that energy.

This is also the way to build wealth: with gratitude and appreciation, and by carefully following a solid wealth management process by using the metrics of the principles of

Modern Portfolio Theory. Building wealth is also about looking at budgeting and where you are spending money, using conservative assumptions, and determining how long your money would last based on those assumptions, the budgeting, and your desired lifestyle. This is planning to solve for the equation of getting from point A to point B. Yet even more important, after all of this planning —assessment, proper diversification, and following the principles and cardinal virtues of portfolio management —is the knowledge of this wonderful common singularity of omnipotence found in all parts of life that I am calling the power of God. This is the light of consciousness behind the witness who watches his or her thoughts. It is the intersection of subject and object, knower and known, and the entire field of knowingness.

> *"The longest journey you will make in your life is from your head to your heart."*
>
> —*Sioux legend*

> *"We rarely hear the inward music, but we are all dancing to it nevertheless."*
>
> —*Rumi, 13th-century Persian poet, jurist, theologian, and Sufi mystic*

Neville Goddard, who wrote a wonderful book called *Awakened Imagination*, said:

> *"Leave the mirror, and change your face. Leave the world alone, and change your perceptions of yourself."*

> *"The moment man discovers that his imagination is Christ, he accomplishes acts which on this level can only be called miraculous. But until man has the sense of Christ as his imagination, he will see everything as pure objectivity without any subjective relationship. Not realizing that all that he encounters is part of himself."*
>
> —*Neville Goddard*

"You did not choose me, I have chosen you."

—*John 15:16*

CONTEMPLATION

Close your eyes, and take a few soft, gentle deep breaths. Hold the empty cup of your heart open in a relaxed and confident way. Open your awareness, and allow yourself to re-experience the Eternal Presence as detailed at the end of Chapter 7. Feel for the burning certainty within you (Supreme Knowing) that you command your destiny. Relax and enjoy the alchemy of heart breath, infinite consciousness, and unshakable intuition of Divine Spirit.

CHAPTER 9

How Would Jesus Occupy Wall Street?

"Do not store up for yourselves treasures on earth, where moth and rust destroy, and where thieves break in and steal. But store up for yourselves treasures in heaven, where moth and rust do not destroy, and where thieves do not break in and steal. For where your treasure is, there your heart will be also."

—*Matthew 6:19-21*

"The sun of truth remains hidden behind the cloud of self-identification with the body."

—*Nisargadatta Maharaj, I Am That*

In the previous two chapters, we discussed several areas of investing and planning to help you better understand how to manage your financial life. In Chapter 7, "The Cardinal Virtues of Intelligent Investing," we offered an outline for the way to manage money properly and use the fundamental portfolio management components. In Chapter 8, "The Yoga of Wealth Management," we talked about how to approach the planning process. We laid the groundwork for how to manage your investments and included a great wealth management process to follow. Now we will bring the deeper focus of the book back into the equation.

WHAT IS "REAL" WEALTH?

Finding Your Way Through the Maze of Suffering

"Don't be afraid that your life will end, be afraid that it will never begin!"

—Anonymous

Even though we may have great success in our professional lives and have built financial wealth, there is still something missing from our lives. Is this not true? This is the premise of the book. We still yearn to fill that void. I have it, many of my friends have it, and if this book resonates with you, then you have it as well. People are suffering. We all suffer; I suffer and you suffer. I want to really get to the point of what it is that is missing from our lives and what are the solutions.

I realized something in my life through this journey, this pain, the suffering, and then the liberation of it, too. This realization was so important to me, and I would like to share some of the things you can do on the journey to cross the rapids of the spiritual river with ease and grace.

What is the path to freedom? What would Krishna tell Arjuna on the battlefield at Kurukshetra? What would the Buddha say to an aspiring Bodhisattva? And how would Jesus speak to Wall Street or one of His disciples?

WHAT IS THE REAL TRUTH?

Taking That Inner Journey

> *"No eye has seen, no ear has heard, and no mind has conceived the things that God has prepared for those who love Him."*
>
> —*1 Corinthians 2:9*

The truth is in the knowing that there's nothing that we perceive outside of ourselves—our wealth, material possessions, status or property—that will fill that hole except for the peace of God. Many never understand that this is, in fact, the actual problem.

Within this book we are appreciating the truth of the great wisdom teachers we spoke about in our previous chapters. Again, we're not focusing just on the dogma of these religions, but rather the spirituality or the actual experience of the truth within the Self, which we can call Atman, Christ consciousness, the Buddha nature, the Tao, or the True Self. Words cannot really do this justice. Once we experience it, many people can't even describe it. Ramana Maharshi sat for two years in silence, incapable of speaking, after his immersion into "The Ocean." We just know it's a union with our Source, a coming home to what we are and where we are from. It is the Yoga of true wealth. No amount of materialism, external quests, or worldly seeking can fulfill us. What our souls are really longing for is God. Only God can satisfy our human cravings.

> *"Jesus answered and said to her, 'Everyone who drinks of this water will thirst again; but whoever drinks of the water that I will give him shall never thirst; but the water that I will give him will become in him a well of water springing up to eternal life.'"*
>
> —*John 4:13-14*

"The kingdom of heaven is like treasure hidden in a field, which someone found and hid; then in his joy he goes and sells all that he has and buys that field."

—Matthew 13:44

"If by giving up limited pleasures one sees far-reaching happiness, the wise one leaves aside limited pleasures, looking to far-reaching happiness."

—Buddha

How do we take the inner journey? Through a disciplined practice of meditation, prayer, giving, loving, and forgiving. A disciplined practice is something that we do every day in our lives. We also need Supreme Knowing: a burning certainty in faith. Knowingness. When we pray, we are not praying for anything other than the grace of God. "Oh, Lord, please come to me. Please be with me. Thy will be done, not mine." We pray for our hearts to understand God's love. We are still.

"Be still and know that I am God."

A solid, regular meditation practice is a tried and tested way of achieving the first essential step on the spiritual path—the stilling of the mind. By stilling the mind, we are shutting down the incessant ego that is chattering all day long. In the normal wakeful consciousness, our agitated, overstimulated minds are attached to the sensory perception of ego. As the Buddha taught, we are stuck in desire and the longings of the sense of I. Meditation allows us to begin to go inward to the Divinity within ourselves. We can do this through several methods, including contemplation, meditation, or meditating on a mantra. We can use audiotapes in the beginning, as well as guided meditations, to help us along. There must be the journey within to look into the Christ consciousness within and to understand the truth of what Jesus said, "The kingdom of heaven is within you," and from Mark 8:36, "For what shall it profit a man, if he shall gain the whole world, and forfeit his soul?" We are taking back our souls in meditation.

Many of us have difficulty in the beginning of a meditation practice due to our mind not stopping its constant thought processes. Do not be discouraged; keep pursuing it. We all have to face our inner darkness; it is an unavoidable aspect of the inner journey and the discovering of the peace of God, the peace that surpasses all understanding.

> *"For I reckon that the sufferings of this present time are not worthy to be compared with the glory which shall be revealed in us."*
>
> —*Romans 8:18*

THE TRUE SELF VS. THE FALSE SELF

Throughout this book, we speak to our audience with great respect, and we're trying to say, "Hey, there is something here. I told you my story. We all have a cross of some kind to bear in this life. I have been successful in business and in life, in general. However, I know that there's something bigger, and it's within us. This is a path to great joy. Through a surrendered state of humility, we become free." It's not like I'm on the mountaintop, talking down to people. I'm saying you can do it, too. You have it in you, if you want it. You have to go inside yourself, strip away the layers of your ego, close your eyes for a substantial time in meditation, and learn how to pray. Really know that there is something within you. Something eternal, divine. I am that. You are that, also. You may not be aware of it, but when you take away all the nonsense, the manmade descriptions, this is who you really are. You are an amazing soul. Within this soul is the True Self.

We only reach it through a tenderhearted stillness, a dissolving of the layers of the ego, the false self, in the presence of perfect love. Ego is the delusion and illusion of who we think we are, combined with what we think this world really is. By increasingly focusing on this inner surrender, we're becoming more of what is called Spirit. We're not just focusing on being materialistic, on wanting and desires, which is what the Buddha described as the cause for all of our sufferings.

Earlier in the book, we talked about the heart of Jesus and building the flame of love within. This is the Sacred Heart. Love is the most potent of all the teachings of Christ, and forgiveness is a major ingredient in the alchemy of perfect love. Once we have achieved a certain degree of surrender to the perfect love within us, then the false self—the ego—does not dominate our sense of Self.

APPROACHES AND DISCIPLINES THAT HELP US

We need a practice to nurture and tenderize the heart. To that end, one of the things I have learned is how important conscious breathing is. We take our breaths for granted. I was so stressed in my job, sometimes I just forgot to breathe. Just being aware of our inhales and exhales can go a long way toward finding peace. Heart-centered breathing on the love of God is a great, simple way to meditate. We quiet our mind when we focus on the breath. We need to take deep, focused breaths. Obviously, everyone realizes, on a rational level, the importance of breathing; however, we really need to focus on inhaling and exhaling, and learn to quiet the mind as we do it. This also takes our mind off the ego mind chatter and puts it on the breath.

Another great technique for reducing stress is alternate nostril breathing: Take three breaths through one nostril while holding closed the other nostril, always alternating nostrils and breaths. I have found this technique, called *nadi shodhan pranayama,* to be extremely effective on my journey into a deepening sense of everlasting peace. Our mind has a tendency to keep regretting or glorifying the past and getting anxious about the future, so this exercise helps to bring the mind back to the present moment.

Science has proven that stress cuts off the compassionate side of our brains. There is nothing more sensitive than a soul. The modern world of war and machines, constant noise and stimulation, traumatizes our souls to varying degrees. A very real consequence of this is that our central nervous system gets stuck in the fight/flight response. Alternate nostril breathing is the fastest and most effective way to disengage it and activate the cool, calm side.

Deep rhythmic breathing also activates the vagus nerve, which provides the digestive, endocrine, and cardiovascular systems with the electricity they need to function optimally. Shallow, stress-based breathing starves our cells of so much oxygen and electricity, and is a chronic situation in our society. Focusing on your breath as much as you can brings countless untold benefits to your life.

An additional wonderful practice is mindful walking. I love my dogs greatly, and one of my favorite things in life is walking my dogs by a river down the street from me. There are many beautiful seabirds, and I just watch the river roll. I try not to think about anything except the beauty I am looking at. As a matter of fact, I am not thinking; I am being. This is total peace, total goodness. I am also totally present to my beautiful dogs. They are present, too. They love the sounds, smells, and sights. Their love is unbelievable. I sense it and hold it in my heart forever. Once in a while, I think about what I am going to feel when my wife and three children, as well as my dogs, part from me, due to the inevitable sorrows of life. This is when I go into the mystic and know that none of us, you included, are ever going to really die. I bury my love for my family, my animals, as well as the whole world, in my heart and hold it there for eternity because I am with God, and they are, too. And then I feel at peace.

This is the wonderful thing about Truth. It truly does set us free.

REFLECTIONS ON THE PEACE OF GOD

In order to be at peace, we need to free others from our consciousness. That means being sorry for any hurts we have caused and asking for forgiveness, not necessarily directly from the harmed ones, but in prayer. If we hold onto discordant thoughts, disharmonies, and memories that we were brought up with and that we received through our DNA from our ancestors, we are clogging our spiritual pores. We can't flow with the peace of God or with the power of God.

This power is much bigger than small self-centeredness and scarcity-minded, fear-based materialism. It's deep in our hearts; we can't build our peace with money. We need very effective forgiveness prayers such as *ho'oponopono* for dissolving the accumulated negativity in the ancestral soul matrix. Most of our ancestors went to their graves full of grievances and disease. And these negative vibrations do not just disappear. Instead, the karmic balance has to be reestablished. The responsibility for this has always passed on through the DNA to the next generation. These are deep and powerful considerations.

One of the most powerful and totally misinterpreted scriptures from the Old Testament alludes to the passing on of discordant karmic energy in the DNA from parents to their children:

> *"I, the Lord thy God, am a jealous and vengeful God visiting the iniquities of the fathers upon the children unto the third and fourth generation."*

> —*Exodus 20:5*

Forgiveness dissolves negative karma. Prayerful ancestral forgiveness dissolves the karma we are carrying in the seed of our souls.

We are one with all things. We have inherited quite literally all the karmic vibrations of our ancestors' thoughts, words, and deeds. They are the very factors that define our genetics. It is wonderful news and extremely liberating to know that through prayer we can literally dissolve whatever negativity and discord exist in the vast reservoir of our psyche and soul. This is really deep stuff, I know, but I also know you are ready for it, or else you would not still be reading this book.

We also should understand God is in everything. God is in the wind, the sun, the plants, the ocean, the trees, the animals, and, of course, ourselves. God is the chirp of the birds, the sound of the train whistle blowing, the bee on a flower, all. The Hindus call this Brahman. If God is in all people, how can we really hate a brother or sister? We might dislike the personality of the ego, but there is a truth of Divinity inside every soul. Every great athlete or rock star or Hollywood star or wealth manager or politician or Olympian —or whatever great talent —should know that God is the doer. The ego personality may think it is the doer, but that is not the true case. Therefore, give the credit to God. Glory be to God. Glory be to Jesus. Glory be to Christ. Thank Buddha. Hare Krishna. Whatever Bhakti yoga you want to practice, it is the spiritual experience that we are after, not the dogma, words, or terms. The Mystical I within us all is the Divinity. When we surrender our ego and trust this power, great things happen.

> "I can do all things through Christ which strengthens me."
>
> —*Philippians 4:13*

We see the deterioration that's been happening in our own society, the egotistical reaching for power, and blind materialism. As we mentioned, no, we're not saying there's anything wrong with building wealth and security; that's what I do for a living. That's what we want to help people do; but as you're building wealth and security, you'll know that there's something bigger— and that is this peace, the peace of God. Surrender everything to God, and know that you don't leave this earth with anything except your soul.

RAISING OUR LEVEL OF CONSCIOUSNESS— STRATEGIES TO HELP

Raising the level of consciousness is a consequence of being centered in the Sacred Heart. This is how Jesus would occupy Wall Street. This is what He would say to us. This is the song of the soul. It is worth repeating: We go through sorrow, we come out of it through prayer and meditation and forgiveness and love. When we come through to the other side, we come to joy. Even sorrows go away. I never knew how to shake the sorrows of life. How could God allow this or that to happen? Once I finally grasped it, that it was my perception of the true nature of reality, then I felt peace. We raise our level of consciousness through prayer, through forgiveness, and through love. All of our world is consciousness. The path to higher peace and insight is through raising our awareness of consciousness.

When we raise our level of consciousness, we don't need material things as a source of fulfillment, because now we sense that the peace within us is greater than anything outside of us could ever bring. That is what we're talking about—offering tools to use to begin to find our way back to where we came from. Returning to love. Returning to God. We came into this world without an appointment through our mother's birth canal, and we believe when we die, that's the end of it. When we understand that there is a part of us that is eternal, it's the truest self that we can ever imagine. Whether it is through the Hindus or Buddhists or the Christians, it is the True Self that we want to find by shedding the ego and letting it go. Letting it all go, we are liberated. Free at last.

The strategies to do this are:

First, we need to acquire some understanding of wisdom teachings. We need to follow some real genuine spiritual practice. I'm not just talking about going to church or becoming vegetarian or rushing through the Our Father and Hail Mary prayers. I'm talking about taking a long look deep inside.

Then we need to start thinking about the people we love and the people we should love that we do not.

We also need to think about how we should let go of our resentments and pride, and about who we should be forgiving that we are not. We can love away the pain. This is where the ho'oponopono prayer, which we discussed in an earlier chapter, will help us. This is a beautiful practice for forgiving everyone and blessing everything. Blessing everything and everyone with love.

You need to find teachings and learn the wisdom and truth. Escape from ignorance. I would tell people to go to the ancient texts that were written 1000, 2000, or 3000 years ago and to really dig into them. We have to read books like the Bible, the Bhagavad Gita, the Dhammapada, the Tao Te Ching. Then we need to find a spiritual discipline that can inspire us to dedicate ourselves to fortifying this transforming self through daily practice, celebration, and prayer.

If we do all of these things, including the meditation and seeking spiritual wisdom from teachings and teachers, something magical happens. A peace will come over us. We are beginning the transformation. Jesus said in Matthew 7:7, "Ask and it will be given to you; seek and you will find; knock and it will be opened to you."

FOUR FORMS OF CONSCIOUSNESS AND OUR NATURAL AWARENESS

> *"Beyond the moving mind there is the background of awareness which does not change."*
>
> —*Sri Nisargadatta Maharaj*

You may recall in Chapter 1 that I told you the story about my mom telling me, "Someday we would swing on a star together," and about her singing to me, "Row, row, row your boat, gently down the stream. Merrily, merrily, merrily, merrily, life is but a dream." The true nature of reality is that there are four main forms of consciousness.

Here are the three that most people are familiar with:

- There's deep sleep when we're not even dreaming
- There's dream sleep
- There's wakefulness

The fourth that most people are not familiar with is known as:

- The Absolute Consciousness

> *"This Alone*
> *Is our Real Nature.*
> *Your duty is to be,*
> *And not to be this or that.*
> *There are no stages in Realization,*
> *Or degrees of Liberation.*
> *There are no levels of Reality;*
> *There are only levels of experience*
> *For the individual.*

If anything can be gained
That was not present before,
It can also be lost.
Whereas the Absolute is eternal,
Here and now.
It is not a matter of becoming,
But of Being."

—*Ramana Maharshi*

TURIYA AND TURIYATITA

Hindu philosophy postulates that there are three alternating levels of relative consciousness: waking, dreaming, and deep sleep. Sri Ramana stated that the Self was the underlying reality that supported the appearance of the other three temporary states. Because of this, he sometimes called the Self *turiya avastha*, or the fourth state. He also occasionally used the word *turiyatita*, meaning "transcending the fourth," to indicate that there are not really four states, but only one true transcendental state.

When we wake up in the morning, it's the wakefulness of the ego. Everyone has ego, and you're never going to stop having that ego completely. But who is to say that this physical world is not just another state of consciousness and that we really are going to return to God at some point and to our true source? Albert Einstein said, "Reality is an illusion, albeit a very persistent one."

We are attached to this material world through the senses, and everything seems so real. When we ask God to come into our life, the pull of form and materialism begins to lose its hold on us. The ego shrinks, and God comes into our hearts. The attachment to the senses falls off, and we become connected to the spirit, the light. That's the end of this dream and the beginning of another level of understanding. Man can't understand it well in this portal because we can't understand God. We are covering up our natural awareness. We have separated over many, many years from our true nature. It is too powerful to understand with all of the ego in the way. We do, however, get a sense of stillness and peace that is greater than anything the false self could ever produce in the form of pleasure.

As we increase our practices and become aware of this natural free state, the illusory world loses its hold on us. We quiet the desirous, wanting mind, and this is the beginning of joy, the beginning of the peace that passes all understanding. We are in joy now, the beginning of the kingdom of heaven within.

SHEDDING THE EGO, NO FEAR, AND FINDING TRUE WISDOM

> *"What we have to recover is our original unity. We have to become what we already are."*
>
> —*Thomas Merton*

Earlier in this book, we offered a few strategies for shedding the ego. But some may find this even more difficult to do because they have become bitter. Some folks become bitter when life gives them pain. This is a shame. We need forgiveness and love and a turning to God. Here we will find the greatest gift of God's grace. Once we shed the ego and belong to God, the freedom and liberation kick in, and we become free birds. Once again, as Rumi's great poem says, "I want to sing like birds sing, not worrying about who is listening or what they think."

The main intention is to see the ego for what it is and move to the heart and the sea of feeling. All of the buildup of disharmony we have been living with can be cleared through love, forgiveness, and prayer. Thoughts and thinking are like the energy, vibrations, and frequency of the material world. Everything is energy. That's what we are from a quantum standpoint, and Einstein proved this. Here we are in this material world as material, as patterns of protons and neutrons. We perceive and we feel that this is reality that we are attached to. We feel our vital senses and our separation from others. We are attached to the illusion of separation from God and we are attached to the dream.

What we are trying to do is go inward to find the true wisdom within through prayer and through meditation, to mold our discordant patterns back into harmony, and to be able to then hear the voice of God and feel the presence of God, and be still.

"Be still and know that I am God."

—*Psalms 46:10*

Do you have fear about the process? FEAR is False Evidence Appearing Real. Much of the whole world is false evidence appearing real. Fear is the epitome of the ego, of the self separate from God. It's called different things in different traditions. Some call it evil and the devil; others just call it the ego or the illusion of the ego. The Buddhists call it Dukkha. The Hindus call it Maya. Fear is a big part of it all. The world is full of fear, among other things. Fear is the absence of love. Remember the premise of the book, *A Course in Miracles:* "Nothing real can be threatened, nothing unreal exists. Herein lies the peace of God."

We are not what we think we are in this body. And the fear is the attachment to the body and mind. We are not our mind or our thoughts. It's beyond thinking, "Here's what you hate." "Here is what I like." It's beyond that. It's a presence within that's like a signal we have to tap into. It's almost like a cable that we have to replug into, to be able to reach it and start to feel it and sense the truth. We develop this frequency by actually eliminating all of the covers to our original truth. The sheaths are what the wonderful Hindus call these covers. That's the cable or frequency of the Self. We are after the Mystical I, the Christ within. You can only get this feeling through God in the heart, not in the mind and thinking it. It is intuition. We need to really get to that point where fear is extinguished through true faith. We need to know the Divine Reality with certainty. We need to die to it all. Surrender the body and mind, the world as we know it. Die to be born again.

THE NEXT DOOR

"Truth is exact correspondence with reality."

—*Paramahansa Yogananda*

Thank you for reading this book. Thank you for recognizing that there is something much more significant than just what is the right process for managing money, the right principles to follow for portfolio management, or the right integration of working with a financial advisor and how to go through the financial plan with confidence. Thank you for realizing that even when we build wealth, there's still something more important—something we all are searching for: to find real wealth.

Many people have a very deep emptiness; it's almost a pain of this emptiness within them, even after having achieved great material successes and financial wealth, even after achieving fame and the respect and admiration of the world. No matter what you achieve with ego consciousness, there is still something missing.

I know you know now that we are not our boats, our cars, our houses, our jets, and our buildings. We are not our hobbies or our friendships, social status, IQ, clothing, accomplishments, none of it. I know you know now that these things will never satisfy the heart and the soul. The Self, as in the True Self, is the eternal blissful Divinity within everyone. This can also be considered the Christ within. To reach it, we just need to eliminate our ego attachment to everything that is not it, which is everything except it. That's why words and dogmas can't describe it. They are just signposts and pointers. There is nothing wrong with having nice things, but when we attach ourselves to them from an identity standpoint, we are on the wrong path. We know Jesus was challenged by His tempters in the desert; He was offered the world.

If you have an emptiness, a hole in your heart, you can fill that hole. If I only had told you how to manage money, it wouldn't have been enough. Because this is what I went through, this is where I came from, this is where I am, and now I know, even when I came through it, I was still clinging to the success and everything. Then you get to another door that you open, you surrender, and you go through it. You say to yourself, "Finally, this is not real, this illusion of myself, of being this person who is so successful." There's much more than this.

If you feel this, let me tell you in Chapter 10 how you can find a way to this other door, this other department, this amazing atonement, the union with God. This is what Jesus taught; this is what Buddha taught. This is the true Yogi experience.

There is some work to be done; everyone is not ready for it, and we know that. This book is for the people who are ready to do the work. This book is for the people who have had the courage to admit, somehow, what we all know deep down in our hearts: material wealth alone is not the prize of Life. The kingdom of heaven is within.

> *"Seek ye first the kingdom of heaven and all these things shall be added unto you."*
>
> —*Matthew 6:33*

> *"Do not search for the truth, only cease to cherish opinions."*
>
> —*Sengstau, 3rd Zen Patriarch*

CONTEMPLATION

Consider deeply the scientific fact and spiritual certainty that we inherit the accumulated vibrations of our ancestors. The sum total of all thoughts, words, and actions coded in the DNA, defining genetics, reverberating in currents along unseen filaments of consciousness bestowing a sobering responsibility— to return the hallowed grounds of the soul to its original state of underlying pristine peace and perfection. Take a few deep breaths, and feel into this truth. What does it mean to you? What feelings does it bring up?

CHAPTER 10

Returning Home

"The eye through which I see God is the same eye through which God sees me; my eye and God's eye are one eye, one seeing, one knowing, one love."

—Meister Eckhart
Christian Mystic
1260-1327
Sermons of Meister Eckhart

"What a liberation to realize that the 'voice in my head' is not who I am. 'Who am I, then?' The one who sees that."

—Eckhart Tolle

"Empty your mind of all thoughts. Let your heart be at peace. Watch the turmoil of beings. Contemplate their return. Each separate being in the universe returns to the common source. Returning to the source is serenity. If you don't realize the source, you stumble in confusion and

sorrow. When you realize where you come from, you naturally become tolerant, disinterested, amused, kindhearted as a grandmother, dignified as a king. Immersed in the wonder of the Tao, you can deal with whatever life brings you, and when death comes, you are ready."

—*Tao Te Ching*
Translation by Stephen Mitchell

In Chapter 9 we summed up the main points of the book and suggested a regular spiritually oriented practice as a means of making progress along the inner path toward the true wealth that exists within us all. The truth of it is that a tremendous resource resides within us all, and the more we access it, the more our lives become fulfilled. Modern civilization's obsessive drive to acquire excessive material wealth as we discussed in Chapter 6 as the Wanting Mind may very well be the externalization of the subconscious yearning to access what lies hidden within.

In this book, I have described this hidden jewel as our true self or the kingdom of heaven. This is actually our own internal connection to Divinity. I believe it is the absence of this connection which causes such painful emptiness, and this is the root cause of much misguided desire such as excessive drinking of alcohol, drugs, shopping, sex, power, as well as an assortment of other frantic pursuits, including becoming obsessed with the accumulation of money. In reality, nothing material can fill a spiritual void.

Although accessing one's inner riches is essentially as simple as relaxing, this simple, natural effortless experience of beingness has become a complicated, mysterious, and mystical thing. That is due to the stress and complexities of life and the complete misdirection of our primary focus outside of ourselves instead of within.

I have discussed how much I love reading Buddhist and Hindu philosophy, especially *Vedanta*, the *Tao Te Ching* and other ancient texts. They have taught me so much wisdom and a greater understanding of the Bible. One of the things I have learned is that God must be sought in earnest. The Hindus taught me the value of a guru. A traditional etymology of the term "guru" is based on the interplay between darkness and light. The guru is seen as the one who "dispels the darkness of ignorance."

I have a deeply personal relationship with, and love for, Jesus. It is not my intention to convert you to Christianity or even use it as a vehicle to promote any religious argument. As the Bible tells us, "The letter kills and the spirit gives life." However, I do enjoy the simple potency of His teachings and the way they dovetail perfectly with the higher wisdom shared from other ancient spiritual traditions. Perhaps you have your own favorite jewels—all shining drops of Truth originating and returning to the same single ocean.

> *"It is easier to pass a camel through the eye of a needle than it is for a rich man to enter the kingdom of heaven."*
>
> *Mark 10:25*

Throughout this book, I have pointed to Jesus having said that the kingdom of heaven is within us. This kingdom is a higher level and a new state of consciousness that transcends all earthly concerns. Within this wisdom I feel it is a simple logical step to realize that when we become overtaken by material, external obligations, we slip into lower levels of consciousness. We all know the more we have to manage, the more time and effort and focus it takes. It is here that we run a great risk in losing not only our inner peace, but our very sense of self.

> *"What does it profit a man if he gaineth the whole world and loses his soul?"*
>
> *Mark 8:36*

Financial planning is my business, and I take it very seriously and enjoy the rewards of success and being a leader in my field. However, I discipline myself to empty my mind and always make time for daily contemplation, meditation, and prayer. In fact, I would honestly say that it is in these "empty" states of consciousness that I enjoy my most profound inspiration and illumination, especially pertaining to the challenges of the world. I also find that deep inner peace is a way of recharging my batteries.

Generally speaking, we have become addicted to stimulation of the senses, and our sense of self has become overidentified with thinking and doing rather than stillness, allowing, and being. The magnificent instrument of our psyches, rather than being like a pure prism for the light of Spirit, has become a distorted projector all tangled with its own misconceptions and seemingly running all of the time.

> *"The mind's reality is a fiction. With that realization, it loses its reign as the arbiter of reality. Through the eye of the ego, life is a kaleidoscope of consciousness-changing attractions and repulsions, fears and transient pleasures."*
>
> —*excerpt from "I-Reality and Subjectivity"*
> *by Dr. David R. Hawkins, M.D., PhD*

Before moving on, I would like to briefly discuss the relative merit of spiritual "practice" versus a faith-based approach to spirituality. Are they mutually beneficial? Do they complement or instead negate each other?

In some cases, faith-based approaches end up being far removed from the experiential nature of spiritual practice. You could look at this as a derivative from the original teachings. Watered down, diluted, and often filled with man-made, ego-based rules and laws that need to be followed to reach some end, somehow consciousness knows that something is missing.

In the case of many Christian-based religions, the many rules of the Old Testament that Jesus had come to simplify have re-emerged and sprung up anew to choke off the power of His original ministry. Remember, Jesus simplified the rule-based religions of His day with statements such as Luke 10:27, "Love the Lord your God with all of your heart and with all of your soul and with all of your strength and with all of your mind" and "Love your neighbor as yourself."

In other situations, our religions and our spiritual practices can thrive, prosper, and grow together. Whether the two complement or negate each other really depends on the experience.

There is no doubt that relinquishing the ego standpoint and embracing a deeper sense of self brings with it tremendous benefit. Life itself, the perfect presence of eternity, holds within it so many riches that it is virtually incomprehensible. As you become more attuned to this presence, more humble to the substance of eternity, tremendous living blessings are infused into your being.

Within this pure, unadulterated, uncontaminated inflow of goodness and enlightened currents of illuminated peace is the living truth of life. These high voltage streams of consciousness can be transformed into human concepts that we can share with others, not just as mere ideas, but as a living presence which we embody.

This embodiment of simple, silent, innocent beingness is the greatest gift we can offer the world. It is the quintessential mythological goal of the hero's journey. The hero returns dripping with a living boon, Jason with the Golden Fleece, Galahad with the Grail, Theseus with the head of the Minotaur, Arthur with Excalibur, David with the head of Goliath—all of these mythological metaphors convey the same eternal truth.

The great spiritual warrior, Jesus of Nazareth, is a fine example of this metaphor. No finer and more potent archetype do we need to consider if we are truly focused on breaking the bonds of the ego's insanity. Kabir has warned us, "Just because the 10,000 lunatics which live in your head have gone quiet, don't think they have left the building." Simply put, it is in the surrendering of self that we find the real peace within us.

Ramana Maharshi, the great Hindu sage, when asked to sum up "The Way," quoted Psalm 46:10: "Be still and know that I am God." The truth is, it's the common threads that come through the Sutras of Pantanjali. It's the great parables of Jesus, and the Dharma from Buddha, and the Tao. It is what God answered to Moses. It is the true jewel that comes through all the great wisdom teachings and truths. One of the truths is that, when we go into silence and just listen and let our minds settle, then our mud can settle, the water can get clear. Then we begin finding our selves.

As the drop relinquishes its mortal sense of self and yields to its intrinsic nature—that of the ocean itself—the very nature of the ocean is revealed. Tremendous relief comes flooding in as we admit to ourselves that the ego, with all of its opinionated positionality based on an inherited sense of separateness, is not only the cause of our stress and woe, but also the root of all obsessive thinking and desire.

> "Thinking proceeds from lack; its purpose is gain. In wholeness, nothing is lacking. All is complete, total, and whole. There is nothing to think about, nor any motive to think. No questions arise, and no answers are sought or needed. Totality is complete, totally fulfilling, with no incompleteness to process."

—Dr. David R. Hawkins, Eye of the I, page 245

Within this book we have continually talked about this internal dysfunction. The Hindus call this dysfunction Maya. Maya, or Māyā (Sanskrit māyā), literally means "illusion." The Buddhist call this dissatisfaction *dukkha*.

The word *dukkha* is significant in Buddhism because of its association with the First Noble Truth—that life is *dukkha*. To understand what the Buddha meant, it's important to understand what *dukkha* means. The word usually is translated into English as "suffering." But it also means temporary, limited, and imperfect. In the Buddhist sense, it refers to anything that is conditioned.

In the Christian tradition, it is called sin. The origin of the word sin really means missing the mark, as in archery. In other words, missing the true point of life.

We are all sinners, according to the Bible; the subtle, often misunderstood reason for this is because we function through the ego sense of self. As we do this, we exist in a state of judgment and fear; in so doing, we miss not only the point of Life but the exquisite feeling of the pure experience of being—the simple joy of living.

LOVE—THE METHOD, THE GOAL, AND THE WAY

It is wonderful news that the magnet with which we can attract this living energy is love itself. Real spiritual practice is an experience of pure and perfect love. The personification of Divinity in the various forms that the world religions revere and adore is a movement toward this loving relationship, but the final step is the revealing of this energy or spirit through our own way of being. When considering a particular practice, one is well advised to consider how simply delightful and delightfully simple a genuine experience can and should be.

A Course in Miracles teaches there is no peace without love and no love without peace. I find that to be a wonderful guideline. There is an utter underlying simplicity in life. It is in simple sweet-hearted receptivity that we can merge with the intrinsic nature of life.

The transformation of the ego nature —from mental concepts, ideology, philosophy, theosophy and religious beliefs into a feeling experience found in silence and inner stillness —is the movement from fear into perfect love. It is through love that the seeds of divine love are watered within us. If we truly love God, then we are required to love ourselves absolutely.

> *"Alexander, Caesar, Charlemagne, and I founded empires. But on what did the creations of our genius rest? Upon force. Jesus alone founded His empire on love, and to this day millions would die for Him."*
>
> —*Napoleon (exiled on St. Helena)*

PERSONAL GOD OR IMPERSONAL PRACTICE?

It is an undeniable fact that much of mainstream Christianity has become a religion of idolatry whereby the idol is being worshipped, instead of the way Jesus championed being walked. When it comes to the spiritual path, there is huge contrast between walking the walk and talking the talk.

However, no matter where your spiritual values lie, a fascinating dance between idea and experience presents itself when your feelings and mind interface. I like to refer to this as an alchemical process to help you to appreciate that a choice need not be made. Within alchemy, it is not a case of this or that or either/or; rather, it is the ratio of ingredients. So what are the ingredients of spiritual experience and practice?

There really are only two ingredients in personal alchemy, and they are thought and feeling. It is the combination of these two critical elements which defines absolutely our entire lives. What most people fail to realize, however, is that self-mastery is a natural consequence and also a prerequisite for walking a successful spiritual path. Self-mastery gives us the ability to change at will the way we think and feel.

This is the first step in aligning us with the love of God. If God is love, and spiritual practice involves relinquishing the ego experience (fear/judgment/separation), then loving oneself puts us on the right track. The story of Jesus is the personification of perfect love. Perfect love, we are told, is the antidote for fear. Fear is the central root of ego. In the story of Jesus we are gifted with perfect love. Perfect love does not require history to validate its potency. Perfect love transcends space/time and all linear concepts of past, present, and future and exists perennially and eternally within the psyche, within the soul. Joseph Campbell, in his exceptional work, *The Hero with a Thousand Faces,* has shed a very bright light on this subject. Whether you question whether Jesus actually walked on this earth, despite the undeniable potency of "the Jesus effect" on history and its multiplicity of historical accounts, it is actually irrelevant. What really matters is, did you get the point of the teaching in the story of perfect love, and are you living in the freedom He brings?

In the core alchemy of the Jesus story there are only two ingredients:

- Faith
- Love

What I have tried to do is present a *tiny taste* of spiritually based teachings that all boil down to the same ingredients and show you that it is these two essential core elements—faith and love—that form the basis of genuine humanity and indeed are the foundation of genuine wealth.

The Jesus story gifts us with a core archetype, personified as a boy who became a man, a revolutionary who stood absolutely against the political and religious systems of the day, and preached a Gospel of absolute simplicity lived out as His very existence itself. Because He was a man who willingly surrendered His own ego for the greater good, He formed a bridge in the psyche of us all. This bridge is a portal deep within the epicenter of our souls, and the journey to it requires a burning faith soaked in the combustible essence of love. It is indeed the ultimate alchemical combination, the merging of which propels us forward through this world in a state of grace.

My prayer for you is that you find these two pillars of faith and love and that God blesses your journey to Him.

> *"I would rather teach one man to pray than ten men to preach."*
>
> —*Charles Spurgeon*

PERFECT LOVE

Luke 15:11-32 New International Version (NIV)
The Parable of the Lost Son

> *"Jesus continued: "There was a man who had two sons.*
>
> *The younger one said to his father, 'Father, give me my share of the estate.' So he divided his property between them.*
>
> *"Not long after that, the younger son got together all he had, set off for a distant country and there squandered his wealth in wild living.*

After he had spent everything, there was a severe famine in that whole country, and he began to be in need.

So he went and hired himself out to a citizen of that country, who sent him to his fields to feed pigs.

He longed to fill his stomach with the pods that the pigs were eating, but no one gave him anything.

When he came to his senses, he said, 'How many of my father's hired servants have food to spare, and here I am starving to death!

I will set out and go back to my father and say to him: Father, I have sinned against heaven and against you.

I am no longer worthy to be called your son; make me like one of your hired servants.'

So he got up and went to his father. But while he was still a long way off, his father saw him and was filled with compassion for him; he ran to his son, threw his arms around him and kissed him.

The son said to him, 'Father, I have sinned against heaven and against you. I am no longer worthy to be called your son.'

But the father said to his servants, 'Quick! Bring the best robe and put it on him. Put a ring on his finger and sandals on his feet.

Bring the fattened calf and kill it. Let's have a feast and celebrate.

For this son of mine was dead and is alive again; he was lost and is found.' So they began to celebrate.

Meanwhile, the older son was in the field. When

he came near the house, he heard music and dancing.

So he called one of the servants and asked him what was going on.

'Your brother has come,' he replied, 'and your father has killed the fattened calf because he has him back safe and sound.'

The older brother became angry and refused to go in. So his father went out and pleaded with him.

But he answered his father, 'Look! All these years I've been slaving for you and never disobeyed your orders. Yet you never gave me even a young goat so I could celebrate with my friends.

But when this son of yours who has squandered your property with prostitutes comes home, you kill the fattened calf for him!'

'My son,' the father said, 'you are always with me, and everything I have is yours.

But we had to celebrate and be glad, because this brother of yours was dead and is alive again; he was lost and is found.'"

TIME TO SAY GOODBYE

I was 27 years old. It was the middle of the night. I had just been called to the hospital because my father had a heart attack. When I arrived, I ran into the room where my father was lying, and he was awake and in great pain. I told him how much I loved him and that everything was going to be all right. Yet he seemed to know something deeper. He said goodbye to me like he was leaving. I told him to stop it, he was going to be fine. In my mind I was thinking that once you made it to the hospital and you were sitting up, everything was going to be all right. He looked at me again much deeper and again said goodbye. I told him again he was going to be fine. Within a few seconds they brought him upstairs to attempt a procedure. But the procedure made him go downhill faster. Hysterical, my four brothers and I began to prepare for the worst.

Our dad died at age 67, a few days later. Once again, I was reminded about what is real in this life. Loving one another. He was such a loving man. He suffered greatly, right up until his last breath. I did have the opportunity to say goodbye as we had a bedside vigil for three days. He may not have understood all that I said to him, but I know he reacted with a sign when I read aloud to him Psalm 23 repeatedly. I said this prayer for three days by his bedside:

> *"The Lord is my Shepherd, I shall not want*
> *He makes me lie down in green pastures*
> *He leads me beside quiet waters. He restores my*
> *soul*
> *Even though I walk through the valley of the*
> *shadow of death,*
> *I will fear no evil for You are with me*
> *Your Rod and Your staff, they comfort me*
> *You prepare a table before me in the presence of*
> *my enemies*
> *You anoint my head with oil, my cup overflows*
> *Surely goodness and love will follow me all the*
> *days of my life*
> *And I dwell in the house of the Lord forever."*

Amen

THE FINAL YOGA

Always discriminate.

When you can distinguish between the Atman and non-Atman, you have reached the culmination of Yoga. As this discrimination grows in the mind of a yogi, he reasons this: I am not this body, which is composed of earth, water, fire, air, and space; and yet clinging to this body, I desire happiness.

Pleasure and pain come and go in the body. Since I am not the body and since in my true nature there is no ebb and flow, I am always the same—serene, peaceful, unmoved by outer events.

Likewise, enjoyment and misery have their beginning and ending in the mind. Since I am not the mind and since my true nature has neither beginning nor end, I am always the same—serene, peaceful, unmoved by inner events. Let pleasure and pain, enjoyment and misery, remain in the body or the mind; it matters nothing to me, for I am the Atman— Existence Knowledge Bliss Absolute.

—*Avadhuta Gita Of Dattatreya*

Eyes of The World

There comes a redeemer, and he slowly too fades away,

And there follows his wagon behind him that's loaded with clay.
And the seeds that were silent all burst into bloom, and decay,
and night comes so quiet, it's close on the heels of the day.

Wake up to find out that you are the eyes of the world,
the heart has its beaches, its homeland and thoughts of its own.
Wake now, discover that you are the song that the mornin' brings,
But the heart has its seasons, its evenin's and songs of its own.[13]

May eternal peace be with you.

---

13   See permission for "Eyes of the World" lyrics in Resources and Permissions section of the book.

EPILOGUE

**Prayer of Freedom
by Howard Wills**

*God, for me, my family, and all humanity
Throughout all time, past, present and future,
Please help us forgive all people
And help us all forgive ourselves.
Please God, thank you, God, Amen.
Help us all Love each other
And Love ourselves,
Be at peace with each other
And be at peace with ourselves.
Please God, thank you, God, Amen.
God, We give you our Love and thank you
For your constant love and blessings,
We appreciate and respect all your creations
And we fill all your creations with our love.
God, we give you our love and thank you
For your constant love and blessings.
We appreciate and respect all of your creations
And we fill all your creations with our love.*

God, please open, bless, empower, expand,
Lead, guide, direct, and protect
Me, my family, and all humanity
Throughout all time
Now and forever.
Please God, thank you, God, Amen
Thank you, God, Amen.

HO'OPONOPONO

Ho'oponopono is the Hawaiian ritual of forgiveness. It proceeds from an understanding of the oneness of everything in the world, which exists even though we feel ourselves to be separate. Because of this oneness, nothing can happen in our own world without creating a resonance in the observer. It follows that we can only influence problems in the external world if we heal the corresponding inner resonance. *Ho'oponopono* consists of four consequent magic sentences: "I am sorry. Please forgive me. Thank you. I love you."

Ho'oponopono: The Hawaiian Forgiveness Ritual
as the Key to Your Life's Fulfillment

Ulrich Emil Duprée

CONTEMPLATION

What is contemplation?
I thought it fitting to give you the definition from a master, Thomas Merton. From his work, *New Seeds of Contemplation* (Burns and Oates, 1999):

> *"Contemplation is the highest expression of our*
> *intellectual and spiritual life. It is that life itself,*
> *fully awake, fully active, fully aware that it is*
> *alive. It is spiritual wonder. It is spontaneous awe*
> *at the sacredness of life, of being. It is gratitude*
> *for life, for awareness and for being. It is a vivid*

realization of the fact that life and being in us proceed from an invisible, transcendent and infinitely abundant source. Contemplation is, above all, awareness of the reality of that source. It knows that source, obscurely, inexplicably, but with a certitude that goes both beyond reason and beyond simple faith."

CENTER OF THE EYE

"In keeping the center of the I empty, the miracle of life can enter and heal."

—*Mark Nepo*

It's not by chance that the dark center of the human eye, the pupil, is actually an empty hole through which the world becomes known to us. Likewise in a spiritual sense, the I is the empty center through which we see everything. It's revealing that such a threshold is called the pupil, for it is only when we are emptied of all noise and dreams of ego that we become truly teachable.

Both the Buddhist and Zen traditions speak of an unbreakable emptiness at the heart of all seeing, like the center of the eye, from which all living things emerge. The Hindu *Upanishads* tell us that in the center of the seed of the great nyagrodha tree, there is nothing, and out of that nothing the great tree grows. We are then reminded that in our time on earth we grow like this tree—out of that nothing. As the essence of the tree is the empty center of its seed, so the essence of our life is the intangible presence at the center of our soul.

Therefore, our chief work as human beings rests in the sincere effort to allow that central presence to inform us. Thus, all forms of prayer and meditation are aimed at keeping the center of the I empty, so the miracle of life in its grace and immensity can enter and heal us.

"Close your eyes and erase the many thoughts and images that arise, one after another, as if your mind is a blackboard and your breath is a

sponge wiping each appearance clean.

Do this until you experience a slowing down of messages. Then open your eyes as if waking for the very first time.

Keep breathing slowly and take in the first thing you see. Feel what is before you. See and feel the wood that makes up the chair next to you and resist preempting its presence by pronouncing it a chair."

—Mark Nepo, The Book of Awakening, *"Center of the Eye," April 8*

"What you are looking for is what is looking."

—St. Francis of Assisi

ST. FRANCIS PRAYER

"Lord, make me an instrument of Your peace. Where there is hatred, let me sow love; where there is injury, pardon; where there is doubt, faith; where there is despair, hope; where there is darkness, light; where there is sadness, joy.
O, Divine Master, grant that I may not so much seek to be consoled as to console; to be understood as to understand; to be loved as to love; For it is in giving that we receive; it is in pardoning that we are pardoned; it is in dying that we are born again to eternal life."

ACKNOWLEDGMENTS AND PERMISSIONS

I would like to thank some special people who made this book possible:

Sydney LeBlanc (SW), Spiritual Warrior, who worked with me on the project. There is no question I could not have completed this without her enthusiasm, guidance, love, and friendship.

Dr. Nick Good, whose insights and friendship have helped me greatly throughout the duration of this project.

John Koehler (The alchemist), who's own faith and love made this publication possible.

Chris Hartpence, Doug Pilley, and Charlotte Twine for copyediting and proofreading help.

Miriam Lerdo, who has been a wonderful assistant of mine at work for the past 22 years and helped me every day during that time.

My friend Jessica Bright for all her help.

My dear friend, Dan Lattanzio, who was overcoming cancer while I was writing this book. With his courage and perseverance, Dan had a miraculous recovery.

My parents, Paul and Catherine. You both were the greatest teachers of love. There is no greater gift in this life than to have parents who teach and express love to their children.

God the Father Almighty, Maker of heaven and Earth. Thank you for all of your grace. Thank you for putting me on this Earth.

Jesus Christ, the son of God, the King of Kings, and my hero and idol. Thank you for being my sacrifice and for showing me "The Way."

Holy Spirit for being with me all along my journey.

Buddha, Krishna, and all the great writers of the Hindu Vedas, as well as Lao Tzu, Ramana Maharshi, and Nisargadatta Maharaj.

We want to thank the Grateful Dead and Ice Nine Publishing Co., Inc. for their permission to include the following song lyrics in the book:

"Box of Rain"
Music by Phillip Lesh, lyrics by Robert Hunter
Copyright © 1970 Ice Nine Publishing Co., Inc.
Copyright renewed.
All rights administered by Universal Music Corp.
(ASCAP)
All rights reserved. Used by permission.

"Unbroken Chain"
Music by Phillip Lesh, lyrics by Robert Peterson
Copyright © 1974 Ice Nine Publishing Co., Inc.
Copyright renewed.
All rights administered by Universal Music Corp.
(ASCAP)
All rights reserved. Used by permission.

CPSIA information can be obtained
at www.ICGtesting.com
Printed in the USA
FFOW04n0834280817
39283FF